The Best of the World's Classics

VOL. III

GREAT BRITAIN AND IRELAND—I

1281—1745

MILTON

BACON

CHAUCER

SHAKESPEARE

THE BEST
OF THE
WORLD'S
CLASSICS

RESTRICTED
TO PROSE

HENRY CABOT LODGE
EDITOR-IN-CHIEF

FRANCIS W. HALSEY
ASSOCIATE EDITOR

With an Introduction, Biographical and Explanatory
Notes, etc.

IN TEN VOLUMES

Vol. III
GREAT BRITAIN AND IRELAND—I

FUNK & WAGNALLS COMPANY
NEW YORK AND LONDON

CONTENTS

CONTENTS

CONTENTS

CONTENTS

CONTENTS

CONTENTS

GREAT BRITAIN AND IRELAND—I

1281—1745

RICHARD DE BURY

Born in 1281, died in 1345; the son of Sir Richard Aungerville, his own name being taken from his birthplace, Bury St. Edmonds; educated at Oxford, and became a Benedictine monk; tutor to Edward III; dean of Wells Cathedral in 1333; bishop of Durham the same year; high chancellor of England in 1334; founded a library at Oxford; his "Philobiblon" first printed at Cologne in 1473.

IN PRAISE OF BOOKS[1]

THE desirable treasure of wisdom and knowledge, which all men covet from the impulse of nature, infinitely surpasses all the riches of the world; in comparison with which, precious stones are vile, silver is clay, and purified gold grains of sand; in the splendor of which, the sun and moon grow dim to the sight; in the admirable sweetness of which, honey and manna are bitter to the taste. The value of wisdom decreaseth not with time; it hath an ever-flourishing virtue that cleanseth its possession from every venom. O celestial gift of divine liberality, descending from the Father of light to raise up the rational soul even to heaven; thou art the celestial alimony of intellect, of which whosoever eateth shall yet hunger, and whoso drinketh shall yet

[1] From the "Philobiblon," a treatise on books, translated from the original Latin into English in 1852 by John Englis. The Latin text and a new translation by Andrew J. West were printed by the Grolier Club of New York in 1887.

3

thirst; a harmony rejoicing the soul of the sorrowful, and never in any way discomposing the hearer. Thou art the moderator and the rule of morals, operating according to which none err. By thee kings reign, and lawgivers decree justly. Through thee, rusticity of nature being cast off, wits and tongues being polished, and the thorns of vice utterly eradicated, the summit of honor is reached and they become fathers of their country and companions of princes, who, without thee, might have forged their lances into spades and plowshares, or perhaps have fed swine with the prodigal son.

Where, then, most potent, most longed-for treasure, art thou concealed? and where shall the thirsty soul find thee? Undoubtedly, indeed, thou hast placed thy desirable tabernacle in books, where the Most High, the Light of light, the Book of Life, hath established thee. There then all who ask receive, all who seek find thee, to those who knock thou openest quickly. In books Cherubim expand their wings, that the soul of the student may ascend and look around from pole to pole, from the rising to the setting sun, from the north and from the south. In them the Most High, Incomprehensible God himself is contained and worshiped. In them the nature of celestial, terrestrial, and infernal beings is laid open. In them the laws by which every polity is governed are decreed, the offices of the celestial hierarchy are distinguished, and tyrannies of such demons are described as the ideas of Plato never surpassed, and the chair of Crito never sustained.

In books we find the dead as it were living;

in books we foresee things to come; in books warlike affairs are methodized; the rights of peace proceed from books. All things are corrupted and decay with time. Satan never ceases to devour those whom he generates, insomuch that the glory of the world would be lost in oblivion, if God had not provided mortals with a remedy in books. Alexander, the ruler of the world; Julius,[2] the invader of the world and the city, the first who in unity of person assumed the empire in arms and arts; the faithful Fabricius,[3] the rigid Cato, would at this day have been without a memorial if the aid of books had failed them. Towers are razed to the earth, cities overthrown, triumphal arches moldered to dust; nor can the king or pope be found, upon whom the privilege of a lasting name can be conferred more easily than by books. A book made renders succession to the author; for as long as the book exists, the author, remaining immortal, can not perish; as Ptolemy witnesseth; in the prolog of his Almagest,[4] he (he says) is not dead, who gave life to science.

What learned scribe, therefore, who draws out things new and old from an infinite treasury of books, will limit their price by any other thing whatsoever of another kind? Truth, overcoming all things, which ranks above kings, wine, and women, to honor which above friends obtains the

[2] The reference is to Julius Cæsar.

[3] The Roman Consul, general and ambassador to Pyrrhus in 280, who was noted for inflexible honesty.

[4] The best-known work of Ptolemy of Alexandria, astronomer and mathematician, who lived in the first half of the second century.

benefit of sanctity, which is the way that deviates not, and the life without end, to which the holy Bœthius attributes a threefold existence in the mind, in the voice, and in writing, appears to abide most usefully and fructify most productively of advantage in books. For the truth of the voice perishes with the sound. Truth, latent in the mind, is hidden wisdom and invisible treasure; but the truth which illuminates books, desires to manifest itself to every disciplinable sense, to the sight when read, to the hearing when heard; it, moreover, in a manner commends itself to the touch, when submitting to be transcribed, collated, corrected, and preserved. Truth confined to the mind, tho it may be the possession of a noble soul, while it wants a companion and is not judged of, either by the sight or the hearing, appears to be inconsistent with pleasure. But the truth of the voice is open to the hearing only, and latent to the sight (which shows as many differences of things fixt upon by a most subtle motion, beginning and ending as it were simultaneously. But the truth written in a book being not fluctuating, but permanent, shows itself openly to the sight passing through the spiritual ways of the eyes, as the porches and halls of common sense and imagination; it enters the chamber of intellect, reposes itself upon the couch of memory, and there congenerates the eternal truth of the mind.

Lastly, let us consider how great a commodity of doctrine exists in books, how easily, how secretly, how safely they expose the nakedness of human ignorance without putting it to shame. These are the masters that instruct us without rods and ferulas, without hard words and anger, without clothes or money. If you approach them, they are not asleep; if investigating you interrogate them, they conceal nothing; if you mistake them, they never grumble, if you are ignorant, they can not laugh at you.

was wont to be called Bezanzon.[8] And there
dwells commonly the Emperor of Greece. And
there is the most fair church and the most noble
of all the world; and it is of Saint Sophie. And
before that church is the image of Justinian the
emperor, covered with gold, and he sits upon a
horse crowned. And he was wont to hold a round
apple of gold in his hand; but it is fallen out
thereof. And men say there, that it is a token
that the emperor has lost a great part of his
lands and of his lordships; for he was wont to
be Emperor of Roumania and of Greece, of all
Asia the less, and of the land of Syria, of the
land of Judea in the which is Jerusalem, and
of the land of Egypt, of Persia, and of Arabia.
But he has lost all but Greece; and that land
he holds all only. And men would many times
put the apple into the image's hand again, but
it will not hold it. This apple betokens the lordship that he had over all the world, that is round.
And the other hand he lifts up against the East,
in token to menace the misdoers. This image
stands upon a pillar of marble at Constantinople.

[8] An old form of the word Byzantium, a town founded by
Megariaus in the seventh century B.C. When Constantine
founded the city to which he gave his own name, Byzantium,
lying east of it, was included within the city limits.

II

AT THE COURT OF THE GREAT CHAN[*]

THE men of Tartary have let make another
city that is called Caydon. And it has twelve
gates, and between the two gates there is always
a great mile; so that the two cities, that is to
say, the old and the new, have in circuit more
than twenty mile.

In this city is the court of the great Chan in
a full great palace and the most passing fair in
all the world, of the which the walls be in circuit more than two mile. And within the walls
it is full of other palaces. And in the garden
of the great palace there is a great hill, upon
the which there is another palace; and it is the
most fair and the most rich that any man may
devise. And all about the palace and the hill
be many trees bearing many diverse fruits. And
all about the hill be ditches great and deep, and
beside them be great fish ponds on that one part
and on that other. And there is a full fair
bridge to pass over the ditches. And in these
vivaries be so many wild geese and ganders
and wild ducks and swans and herons that it
is without number. And all about these ditches
and vivaries is the great garden full of wild
beasts. So that when the great Chan will have
any disport on that, to take any of the wild
beasts or of the fowls, he will let chase them and

[*] From the "Travels."

11

take them at the windows without going out of his chamber.

This palace, where his court is, is both great and passing fair. And within the palace, in the hall, there be twenty-four pillars of fine gold. And all the walls be covered within of red skins of beasts that men call panthers, that be fair beasts and well smelling; so that for the sweet odor of those skins no evil air may enter into the palace. Those skins be as red as blood, and they shine so bright against the sun, that scarcely no man may behold them. And many folk worship these beasts, when they meet them first at morning, for their great virtue and for the good smell that they have. And those skins they prize more than tho they were plate of fine gold.

And in the midst of this palace is the reservoir for the great Chan, that is all wrought of gold and of precious stones and great pearls. And at four corners of the reservoir be four serpents of gold. And all about there is made large nets of silk and gold and great pearls hanging all about the reservoir. And under the reservoir be conduits of beverage that they drink in the emperor's court. And beside the conduits be many vessels of gold, by the which they that be of household drink at the conduit.

And the hall of the palace is full nobly arrayed, and full marvellously attired on all parts in all things that men apparel with any hall. And first, at the chief of the hall is the emperor's throne, full high, where he sits at the meat. And that is of fine precious stones, bordered all about with pure gold and precious stones, and great pearls. And the steps that he goes up to the table be of precious stones mingled with gold.

And at the left side of the emperor's seat is the seat of his first wife, one degree lower than the emperor; and it is of jasper, bordered with gold and precious stones. And the seat of his second wife is also another seat more lower than his first wife; and it is also of jasper, bordered with gold, as that other is. And the seat of the third wife is also more low, by a degree, than the second wife. For he has always three wives with him, where that ever he be.

And after his wives, on the same side, sit the ladies of his lineage yet lower, after that they be of estate. And all those that be married have a counterfeit made like a man's foot upon their heads, a cubit long, all wrought with great pearls, fine and orient, and above made with peacocks' feathers and of other shining feathers; and that stands upon their heads like a crest, in token that they be under man's foot and under subjection of man. And they that be unmarried have none such.[10]

[10] The quaint words in which "Mandeville" concludes his book are these: "And I, John Mandeville, knight, above said (altho I be unworthy), that departed from our countries and passed the sea, the year of grace a thousand three hundred and twenty-two, that have passed many lands and many isles and countries, and searched many full strange places, and have been in many a full good honorable company, and at many a fair deed of arms (albeit that I did none myself, for mine unable insuffisance), now I am come home, in spite of myself, to rest, for gouts arthritic that me distrain, that define the end of my labor; against my will (God knows)."

JOHN WYCLIF

Born about 1324, died in 1384; "The Morning Star of the Reformation"; educated at Oxford; rector in Lincolnshire and Buckinghamshire; Royal ambassador to papal nuncios at Bruges in 1374; in sermons attacked the Church of Rome; five papal bulls, authorizing his imprisonment, signed against him; threw off allegiance to the Church and wrote fearlessly against papal claims; died of paralysis; his bones in 1428 exhumed and burnt and his ashes cast into the river Swift by order of the synod of Constance; his translation of the Bible from the Vulgate, completed about 1382, was the first complete translation ever made.

THE BAPTISM OF CHRIST[1]

1 The bigynnynge of the gospel of Jhesu Crist, the sone of God.

2 As it is writun in Ysaie, the prophete, Lo! I send myn angel bifore thi face, that schal make thi weye redy before thee.

3 The voyce of oon cryinge in desert, Make ye redy the weye of the Lord, make ye his pathis rihtful.

4 Jhon was in desert baptisynge, and prechinge the baptym of penaunce, into remiscioun of synnes.

5 And alle men of Jerusalem wenten out to him, and al the cuntree of Judee; and weren baptisid

---

[1] Part of Chapter I of the Gospel of St. Mark, as translated by Wyclif. It will be noted that Wyclif's orthography is irregular, the same word being often spelled differently on the same page. This selection is printed in the original as a specimen of the English of Wyclif's time.

of him in the flood of Jordan, knowlechinge her synnes.

6 And John was clothid with heeris of camelis, and a girdil of skyn abowte his leendis; and he eet locusts, and hony of the wode, and prechide, seyinge:

7 A strengere than I schal come aftir me, of whom I knelinge am not worthi for to vndo, *or vnbynde*, the thwong of his schoon.

8 I have baptisid you in water; forsothe he shal baptise you in the Holy Goost.

9 And it is don in thoo dayes, Jhesus came fro Nazareth of Galilee, and was baptisid of Joon in Jordan.

10 And anoon he styinge vp of the water, sayth heuenes openyd, and the Holy Goost cummynge doun as a culuere, and dwellynge in hym.

11 And a voys is maad fro heuenes, thou art my sone loued, in thee I haue plesid.

12 And anon the Spirit puttide hym in to desert.

13 And he was in desert fourty dayes and fourty nightis, and was temptid of Sathanas, and was with beestis and angelis mynstriden to hym.

14 Forsothe aftir that Joon was taken, Jhesus came in to Galilee, prechinge the gospel of the kyngdam of God,

15 And seiynge, For tyme is fulfillid, and the kyngdam of God shal come niy; forthinke yee, *or do yee penaunce*, and bileue yee to the gospel.

16 And he passynge bisidis the see of Galilee, say Symont, and Andrew, his brother, sendynge nettis into the see; sothely thei weren fishers.

17 And Jhesus seide to hem, Come yee after me; I shal make you to be maad fishers of men.

For these causes, saith Cato, waketh and inclineth you not over much to sleep, for over much rest nourisheth and causeth many vices; and therefore saith St. Jerome: Do some good deeds, that the devil, which is our enemy, find you not unoccupied, for the devil he taketh not lightly unto his working such as he findeth occupied in good works.

Then thus in getting riches ye must flee idleness; and afterward ye should use the riches which ye have got by your wit and by your travail, in such manner, that men hold you not too scarce, nor too sparing, nor fool-large, that is to say, over large a spender; for right as men blame an avaricious man because of his scarcity and niggardliness, in the same wise he is to blame that spendeth over largely; and therefore saith Cato: Use (saith he) the riches that thou hast obtained in such manner, that men have no matter nor cause to call thee neither wretch nor miser, for it is a great shame to a man to have a poor heart and a rich purse; he saith also: The goods that thou hast obtained, use 'em by measure, that is to say, spend measurably, for they that foolishly waste and squander the goods that they have, when they have no more proper of 'eir own, that they prepare to take the goods of another man. I say, then, that ye should flee avarice, using your riches in such manner, that men say not that your riches are buried, but that ye have 'em in your might and in your wielding; for a wise man reproveth the avaricious man, and saith thus in two verse: Whereto and why burieth a man his goods by his great avarice, and knoweth well that needs must he die, for death is the end of every man as in this present life.

And for what cause or reason joineth he him, or knitteth he him so fast unto his goods, that all his wits will not dissever him or depart him from his goods, and knoweth well, or ought to know, that when he is dead he shall nothing bear with him out of this world? And therefore saith St. Augustine, that the avaricious man is likened unto hell, that the more it swalloweth the more desire it hath to swallow and devour. And as well as ye would eschew to be called an avaricious man or a chinch, as well should ye keep you and govern you in such wise, that men call you not fool-large; therefore, saith Tullius: The goods of thine house should not be hid nor kept so close, but that they might be opened by pity and debonnairety, that is to say, to give 'em part that have great need; but the goods should not be so open to be every man's goods.

WILLIAM CAXTON

Born about 1422, died in 1491; the first English printer; began to translate the "Histories de Troye" in 1469 and issued the work in 1474, either at Cologne or Bruges; translated and had printed in 1475 "The Game and Playe of Chesse," the second printed English book; set up a press in Westminster, London, in 1476, where he continued to print books until his death.

OF TRUE NOBILITY AND CHIVALRY[1]

THE knight ought to be made all armed upon an apt horse, in such wise that he have an helmet on his head, and a spear in his right hand, and covered with his shield; a sword and a mace on his left side; clad with an hauberk and plates before his breast; leg harness on his legs; spurs on his heels; on his hands his gauntlets. His horse well broken and taught, and apt to battle, and covered with his arms. When the knights be made they be bayned or bathed. That is the sign that they should lead a new life and new manners; also they wake all the night in prayers and orisons unto God that he will give them grace that they may get that thing that they may not get by nature. The king or prince girdeth about them a sword, in sign that they should abide and keep him of whom they take their dispences and dignity.

Also a knight ought to be wise, liberal, true, strong, and full of mercy and pity, and keeper of the people, and of the law, and right as chivalry passeth other in virtue, in dignity, in honor,

[1] From the "Game and Playe of Chesse," translated by Caxton from the French original.

22

and in reverence, right so ought he to surmount all other in virtue; for honor is nothing else but to do reverence to another person for the good and virtuous disposition that is in him. A noble knight ought to be wise and proved before he be made knight; it behoveth him that he had long time used the war and arms; that he may be expert and wise for to govern others. For since a knight is captain of a battle, the life of them that shall be under him lieth in his hand, and therefore behooveth him to be wise and well advised. For sometimes art, craft and engine is more worth than strength of hardiness of a man that is not proved in arms, for otherwhile it happeneth that when the prince of the battle relies on and trusteth in his hardiness and strength, and will not use wisdom and engine for to run upon his enemies, he is vanquished and his people slain. Therefore saith the philosopher that no man should choose young people to be captains and governors, forasmuch as there is no certainty in their wisdom. Alexander of Macedon vanquished and conquered Egypt, Judæa, Chaldee, Africa, and Assyria unto the marches of Bragmans more by the counsel of old men than by the strength of the young men.

The very true love of the common weal and profit nowadays is seldom found. Where shalt thou find a man in these days that will expose himself for the worship and honor of his friend or for the common weal. Seldom or never shall he be found. Also the knights should be large and liberal, for when a knight hath regard unto his singular profit by his covetousness, he despoileth his people. For when the soldiers see

that they put them in peril, and their master
will not pay them their wages liberally, but intendeth to his own proper gain and profit, then,
when the enemies come, they turn soon their
backs and flee oftentimes. And thus it happeneth by him that intendeth more to get money
than victory, that his avarice is ofttimes cause
of his confusion.

Then let every knight take heed to be liberal,
in such wise that he ween not nor suppose that
his scarcity be to him a great winning or gain.
And for this cause he be the less loved of his
people, and that his adversary withdraw to him
them by large giving. For ofttime battle is advanced more for getting of silver than by the
force and strength of men. For men see all day
that such things as may not be achieved by force
of nature be gotten and achieved by force of
money. And forsomuch it behooveth to see well
to that when the time of battle cometh, that he
borrow not, nor make no curtailment. For no
man may be rich that leaveth his own, hoping
to get and take of others. Then alway all their
gain, and winning ought to be common among
them except their arms. For in like wise as the
victory is common, so should the despoil and
booty be common unto them. And therefore
David, that gentle knight in the first book of
Kings in the last chapter, made a law: that he
that abode behind by malady or sickness in the
tents should have as much part of the booty as
he that had been in the battle. And for the love
of this law he was made afterward king of Israel.

Alexander of Macedon came in a time like a
simple knight unto the court of Porus, king of

Ind, for to espy the estate of the king and of
the knights of the court. And the king received
him right worshipfully and demanded many
things of Alexander and of his constancy and
strength, nothing weening that he had been Alexander, but Antigone, one of his knights. And
after he had him to dinner; and when they had
served Alexander in vessel of gold and silver
with diverse meats, after that he had eaten such
as pleased him, he voided the meat and took the
vessel and held it to himself and put it in his bosom
or sleeves. Whereof he was accused unto the
king. After dinner then the king called him and
demanded wherefore he had taken his vessel, and
he answered: Sir King, my lord, I pray thee to
understand and take heed thyself and also thy
knights. I have heard much of thy great high-
ness, and that thou art more mighty and puissant
in chivalry and in dispences than is Alexander,
and therefore I am come to thee, a poor knight,
which am named Antigone, for to serve thee.
Then it is the custom in the court of Alexander
that what thing a knight is served with, all is
his, meat and vessel and cup. And therefore
I had supposed that this custom had been kept
in thy court, for thou art richer than he. When
the knights heard this, anon they left Porus, and
went to serve Alexander, and thus he drew to him
the hearts of them by gifts, which afterward slew
Porus that was king of Ind, and they made Alexander king thereof. Therefore remember, knight,
alway that with a closed and shut purse thou
shalt never have victory. Ovid saith that he that
taketh gifts, he is glad therewith, for they win
with gifts the hearts of the gods and of men.

SIR THOMAS MALORY

Born about 1430, died after 1470; compiler and translator
of the "Morte d'Arthur" from French prose romances which
had been built up on earlier poems dealing with the life and
death of King Arthur and the knights of the Round Table;
the "Morte d'Arthur" printed by Caxton in 1485.

OF THE FINDING OF A SWORD FOR ARTHUR[1]

AND so Merlin and he departed, and as they
rode King Arthur said, "I have no sword." "No
matter," said Merlin; "hereby is a sword that
shall be yours and I may." So they rode till
they came to a lake, which was a fair water and
a broad; and in the midst of the lake King
Arthur was aware of an arm clothed in white
samite, that held a fair sword in the hand. "Lo,"
said Merlin unto the King, "yonder is the sword
that I spake of."

With that they saw a damsel going upon the
lake. "What damsel is that?" said the King.
"That is the Lady of the Lake," said Merlin;
"and within that lake is a reach, and therein
is as fair a place as any is on earth, and richly
beseen; and this damsel will come to you anon,
and then speak fair to her that she will give you
that sword." Therewith came the damsel to

[1] From the "Morte d'Arthur."

26

King Arthur, and saluted him, and he her again. "Damsel," said the King, "what sword is that which the arm holdeth yonder above the water? I would it were mine, for I have no sword." "Sir King," said the damsel of the lake, "that sword is mine, and if ye will give me a gift when I ask it you, ye shall have it." "By my faith," said King Arthur, "I will give you any gift that you will ask or desire." "Well," said the damsel, "go ye into yonder barge, and row yourself unto the sword, and take it and the scabbard with you; and I will ask my gift when I see my time."

So King Arthur and Merlin alighted, tied their horses to two trees, and so they went into the barge. And when they came to the sword that the hand held, King Arthur took it up by the handles, and took it with him; and the arm and the hand went under the water, and so came to the land and rode forth.

Then King Arthur saw a rich pavilion. "What signifieth yonder pavilion?" "That is the knight's pavilion that ye fought with last—Sir Pellinore; but he is out; for he is not there: he hath had to do with a knight of yours, that hight Eglame, and they have foughten together a great while, but at the last Eglame fled, and else he had been dead; and Sir Pellinore hath chased him to Carlion, and we shall anon meet with him in the highway." "It is well said," quoth King Arthur; "now have I a sword, and now will I wage battle with him and be avenged on him." "Sir, ye shall not do so," said Merlin: "for the knight is weary of fighting and chasing; so that ye shall have no worship to have a do with him. Also he will not lightly be matched of one knight living: and therefore my counsel is, that yet let him pass; for he shall do you good service in short time, and his sons after his days. Also ye shall see that day in short space, that ye shall be right glad to give him your sister to wife." "When I see him," said King Arthur, "I will do as ye advise me."

Then King Arthur looked upon the sword and liked it passing well. "Whether liketh you better," said Merlin, "the sword or the scabbard?" "Me liketh better the sword," said King Arthur. "Ye are more unwise," said Merlin; "for the scabbard is worth ten of the sword: for while ye have the scabbard upon you, ye shall lose no blood, be ye never so sore wounded—therefore keep well the scabbard alway with you." So they rode on to Carlion.

SIR THOMAS MORE

Born in 1478, died in 1535; met Erasmus in London in 1497; after 1503 devoted himself mainly to politics; entered Parliament in 1504; ambassador to Flanders in 1515; published "Utopia" in 1516; privy counsellor to Henry VIII in 1518; present with the King at the Field of the Cloth of Gold in 1520; speaker of the House of Commons in 1523; defended the papacy against Luther; succeeded Wolsey as chancellor in 1529; refused in 1534 to take the oath of adherence to the act vesting the succession in the issue of Anne Boleyn and committed to the Tower, indicted for high treason and executed July 6th, 1535.

LIFE IN UTOPIA [1]

THERE are fifty-four cities in the island, all large and well built, the manners, customs, and laws of which are the same, and they are all contrived as near in the same manner as the ground on which they stand will allow. The nearest lie at least twenty-four miles' distance from one another, and the most remote are not so far distant but that a man can go on foot in one day from it to that which lies next it. Every city sends three of their wisest senators once a year to Amaurot, to consult about their common concerns; for that is the chief town of the island, being situated near the center of it, so that it

[1] The "Utopia" was written originally in Latin. It derived its name from an imaginary island, the seat of an ideal state. Ralph Robinson made a translation into English in 1551. Another translation was made by Bishop Burnet in 1683.

is the most convenient place for their assemblies. The jurisdiction of every city extends at least twenty miles; and where the towns lie wider, they have much more ground. No town desires to enlarge its bounds, for the people consider themselves rather as tenants than landlords.

They have built, over all the country, farm-houses for husbandmen; which are well contrived, and furnished with all things necessary for country labor. Inhabitants are sent, by turns, from the cities to dwell in them; no country family has fewer than forty men and women in it, besides two slaves. There is a master and a mistress set over every family, and over thirty families there is a magistrate. Every year twenty of this family come back to the town after they have stayed two years in the country, and in their room there are other twenty sent from the town, that they may learn country work from those that have been already one year in the country, as they must teach those that come to them the next from the town. By this means such as dwell in those country farms are never ignorant of agriculture, and so commit no errors which might otherwise be fatal and bring them under a scarcity of corn. But tho there is every year such a shifting of the husbandmen, to prevent any man being forced against his will to follow that hard course of life too long, yet many among them take such pleasure in it that they desire leave to continue in it many years.

These husbandmen till the ground, breed cattle, hew wood and convey it to the towns either by land or water, as is most convenient. They breed an infinite multitude of chickens in a very

curious manner: for the hens do not sit and
hatch them, but a vast number of eggs are laid
in a gentle and equal heat in order to be hatched;
and they are no sooner out of the shell, and able
to stir about, but they seem to consider those
that feed them as their mothers, and follow them
as other chickens do the hen that hatched them.
They breed very few horses, but those they have
are full of mettle, and are kept only for exer-
cising their youth in the art of sitting and riding
them; for they do not put them to any work,
either of plowing or carriage, in which they em-
ploy oxen. For tho their horses are stronger,
yet they find oxen can hold out longer; and as
they are not subject to so many diseases, so they
are kept upon a less charge and with less trouble.
And even when they are so worn out that they
are no more fit for labor, they are good meat at
last. They sow no corn but that which is to
be their bread: for they drink either wine, cider,
or perry, and often water, sometimes boiled with
honey or licorice, with which they abound; and
tho they know exactly how much corn will serve
every town and all that tract of country which
belongs to it, yet they sow much more, and breed
more cattle, than are necessary for their con-
sumption, and they give that overplus of which
they make no use to their neighbors.

When they want anything in the country which
it does not produce, they fetch that from the
town, without carrying anything in exchange for
it. And the magistrates of the town take care
to see it given them; for they meet generally in
the town once a month, upon a festival day.
When the time of harvest comes, the magistrates

in the country send to those in the towns, and
let them know how many hands they will need
for reaping the harvest; and the number they
call for being sent to them, they commonly dispatch it all in one day.

He that knows one of their towns knows them
all—they are so like one another, except where
the situation makes some difference. I shall
therefore describe one of them, and none is so
proper as Amaurot; for as none is more eminent
(all the rest yielding in precedence to this, because it is the seat of their supreme council),
so there was none of them better known to me,
I having lived five years all together in it.

It lies upon the side of a hill, or rather a rising
ground. Its figure is almost square: for from
the one side of it, which shoots up almost to the
top of the hill, it runs down in a descent for
two miles, to the river Anider; but it is a little
broader the other way that runs along by the
bank of that river. The Anider rises about
eighty miles above Amaurot, in a small spring
at first. But other brooks falling into it, of
which two are more considerable than the rest,
as it runs by Amaurot it is grown half a mile
broad; but it still grows larger and larger, till
after sixty miles' course below it, it is lost in
the ocean. Between the town and the sea, and
for some miles above the town, it ebbs and flows
every six hours with a strong current. The tide
comes up about thirty miles so full that there
is nothing but salt water in the river, the fresh
water being driven back with its force; and above
that, for some miles, the water is brackish; but
a little higher, as it runs by the town, it is quite

fresh; and when the tide ebbs, it continues fresh all along to the sea. There is a bridge cast over the river, not of timber, but of fair stone, consisting of many stately arches; it lies at that part of the town which is farthest from the sea, so that the ships, without any hindrance, lie all along the side of the town.

There is likewise another river that runs by it, which, tho it is not great, yet it runs pleasantly, for it rises out of the same hill on which the town stands, and so runs down through it and falls into the Anider. The inhabitants have fortified the fountain-head of this river, which springs a little without the towns; that so, if they should happen to be besieged, the enemy might not be able to stop or divert the course of the water, nor poison it; from thence it is carried in earthen pipes to the lower streets. And for those places of the town to which the water of that small river can not be conveyed, they have great cisterns for receiving the rain-water, which supplies the want of the other.

The town is compassed with a high and thick wall, in which there are many towers and forts; there is also a broad and deep dry ditch, set thick with thorns, cast round three sides of the town, and the river is instead of a ditch on the fourth side. The streets are very convenient for all carriage, and are well sheltered from the winds. Their buildings are good, and are so uniform that a whole side of a street looks like one house. The streets are twenty feet broad. There lie gardens behind all their houses; these are large, but inclosed with buildings, that on all hands face the streets, so that every house has both a door to the street and a back door to the garden. Their doors have all two leaves, which, as they are easily opened, so they shut of their own accord; and there being no property among them, every man may freely enter into any house whatsoever. At every ten years' end they shift their houses by lots. They cultivate their gardens with great care, so that they have both vines, fruits, herbs, and flowers in them; and all is so well ordered and so finely kept that I never saw gardens anywhere that were both so fruitful and so beautiful as theirs. And this humor of ordering their gardens so well is not only kept up by the pleasure they find in it, but also by an emulation between the inhabitants of the several streets, who vie with each other. And there is, indeed, nothing belonging to the whole town that is both more useful and more pleasant. So that he who founded the town seems to have taken care of nothing more than of their gardens; for they say the whole scheme of the town was designed at first by Utopus, but he left all that belonged to the ornament and improvement of it to be added by those that should come after him, that being too much for one man to bring to perfection.

Their records, that contain the history of their town and state, are preserved with an exact care, and run backward seventeen hundred and sixty years. From these it appears that their houses were at first low and mean, like cottages, made of any sort of timber, and were built with mud walls and thatched with straw. But now their houses are three stories high; the fronts of them are faced either with stone, plastering, or brick,

and between the facings of their walls they throw
in their rubbish. Their roofs are flat; and on
them they lay a sort of plaster, which costs very
little, and yet is so tempered that it is not apt
to take fire, and yet resists the weather more
than lead. They have great quantities of glass
among them, with which they glaze their windows; they use also in their windows a thin linen
cloth, that is so oiled or gummed that it both
keeps out the wind and gives free admission to
the light.

JOHN KNOX

Born in 1505, died in 1572; early influenced by George
Wishart, a Lutheran refugee who had found an asylum
in Scotland; a royal chaplain in 1550; assisted in the
revision of the Prayer-book; fled to the Continent after
the accession of Mary Tudor and visited Calvin; preached
for a time at Frankfort and afterward traveled and preached
in Scotland; occupied himself with the organization of the
Presbyterian Church, having frequent dramatic encounters
with Mary, Queen of Scots, whose sympathies were Catholic.

AN INTERVIEW WITH MARY, QUEEN
OF SCOTS[1]

THE queen, in a vehement fume, began to cry
out that never prince was handled as she was.
"I have," said she, "borne with you in all your
rigorous manner of speaking, both against myself
and against my uncles; yea, I have sought your
favors by all possible means. I offered unto
you presence and audience, whensoever it pleased
you to admonish me, and yet I cannot be quit of
you. I avow to God I shall be anes [once]
revenged." And with these words scarcely could

[1] From the "History of the Reformation in Scotland."
The spelling has been modernized. After the arrival of
Mary in Scotland in 1561, Knox had several interviews
with her, followed by an open rupture with her party in
the government of Scotland, and by his retirement into com-
parative privacy. Burton, the historian of Scotland, believes
that the dialog here given took place in French, rather than
in the language in which Knox reports it. Mary's habitual
speech was French and Knox knew the language well.

Marnock, her secret chamber-boy, get napkins to hold her eyes dry for the tears; and the owling, besides womanly weeping, stayed her speech.

The said John did patiently abide all the first fume, and at opportunity answered: "True it is, Madam, your Grace and I have been at diverse controversies, into the which I never perceived your Grace to be offended at me. But when it shall please God to deliver you from that bondage of darkness and error, in the which ye have been nourished, for the lack of true doctrine, your majesty will find the liberty of my tongue nothing offensive. Without the preaching-place, Madam, I think few have occasion to be offended at me, and there, Madam, I am not master of myself, but man [must] obey Him who commands me to speak plain, and to flatter no flesh upon the face of the earth."

"But what have ye to do," said she, "with my marriage?"

"If it please your majesty," said he, "patiently to hear me, I shall shew the truth in plain words. I grant your Grace offered me more than ever I required; but my answer was then, as it is now, that God hath not sent me to await upon the courts of princesses, nor upon the chambers of ladies; but I am sent to preach the evangel of Jesus Christ to such as please to hear it; and it hath two parts—repentance and faith. And now, Madam, in preaching repentance, of necessity it is, that the sins of men be so noted, that they may know wherein they offend; but so it is, that the most part of your nobility are so addicted to your affections, that neither God, His word, nor yet their commonwealth, are rightly

ROGER ASCHAM

Born in 1515, died in 1568; educated at Cambridge, where he taught Greek; became a tutor to Princess Elizabeth, afterward to the Queen, in 1548; served as Latin Secretary to Queens Mary and Elizabeth, 1563-68; his work, "The Schoolmaster," published in 1570.

OF GENTLE METHODS IN TEACHING[a]

YET some will say that children, of nature, love pastime, and mislike learning; because, in their kind, the one is easy and pleasant, the other hard and wearisome. Which is an opinion not so true as some men ween. For the matter lieth not so much in the disposition of them that be young, as in the order and manner of bringing up by them that be old; nor yet in the difference of learning and pastime. For, beat a child if he dance not well, and cherish him tho he learn not well, you shall have him unwilling to go to dance, and glad to go to his book; knock him always when he draweth his shaft ill, and favor him again tho he fault at his book, you shall have him very loth to be in the field, and very willing to be in the school. Yea, I say more, and not of myself, but by the judgment of those from whom few wise men will gladly dissent; that if ever the nature of man be given at any time, more than other, to receive goodness, it is in innocency of young years, before that experience of evil have taken root in him. For the

[a] From "The Schoolmaster."

40

pure clean wit of a sweet young babe is like the newest wax, most able to receive the best and fairest printing; and like a new bright silver dish never occupied, to receive and keep clean any good thing that is put into it.

And thus, will in children, wisely wrought withal, may easily be won to be very well willing to learn. And wit in children, by nature, namely memory, the only key and keeper of all learning, is readiest to receive and surest to keep any manner of thing that is learned in youth. This, lewd and learned, by common experience know to be most true. For we remember nothing so well when we be old as those things which we learned when we were young. And this is not strange, but common in all nature's works. "Every man seeth (as I said before) new wax is best for printing, new clay fittest for working, new-shorn wool aptest for soon and surest dyeing, new fresh flesh for good and durable salting." And this similitude is not rude, nor borrowed of the larder-house, but out of his school-house, of whom the wisest of England need not be ashamed to learn. "Young grafts grow not only soonest, but also fairest, and bring always forth the best and sweetest fruit; young whelps learn easily to carry; young popinjays learn quickly to speak." And so, to be short, if in all other things, tho they lack reason, sense, and life, the similitude of youth is fittest to all goodness, surely nature in mankind is most beneficial and effectual in their behalf.

Therefore, if to the goodness of nature be joined the wisdom of the teacher, in leading young wits into a right and plain way of learning; surely children kept up in God's fear, and governed by His grace, may most easily be brought well to serve God and their country, both by virtue and wisdom.

But if will and wit, by farther age, be once allured from innocency, delighted in vain sights, filled with foul talk, crooked with wilfulness, hardened with stubbornness, and let loose to disobedience; surely it is hard with gentleness, but impossible with severe cruelty, to call them back to good frame again. For where the one perchance may bend it, the other shall surely break it: and so, instead of some hope, leave an assured desperation, and shameless contempt of all goodness; the furthest point in all mischief, as Xenophon doth most truly and most wittily mark.

Therefore, to love or to hate, to like or to contemn, to ply this way or that way to good or to bad, ye shall have as ye use a child in his youth.

And one example whether love or fear doth work more in a child for virtue and learning, I will gladly report; which may be heard with some pleasure, and followed with more profit.

Before I went into Germany, I came to Broadgate in Leicestershire, to take my leave of that noble lady, Jane Grey, to whom I was exceeding much beholding. Her parents, the duke and duchess, with all the household, gentlemen and gentlewomen, were hunting in the park. I found her in her chamber, reading Phædo Platonis in Greek, and that with as much delight as some gentlemen would read a merry tale in Boccace. After salutation and duty done, with some other talk, I asked her why she would leese [lose] such pastime in the park? Smiling she answered me: "I wisse, all their sport in the park is but a shadow to that pleasure that I find in Plato. Alas! good folk, they never felt what true pleasure meant." "And how came you, madame," quoth I, "to this deep knowledge of pleasure? and what did chiefly allure you unto it, seeing not many women, but very few men, have attained thereunto?" "I will tell you," quoth she, "and tell you a truth, which perchance ye will marvel at. One of the greatest benefits that ever God gave me, is, that He sent me so sharp and severe parents, and so gentle a schoolmaster. For when I am in presence either of father or mother, whether I speak, keep silence, sit, stand, or go, eat, drink, be merry, or sad, be sewing, playing, dancing, or doing anything else, I must do it, as it were, in such weight, measure, and number, even so perfectly, as God made the world; or else I am so sharply taunted, so cruelly threatened, yea, presently, sometimes with pinches, nibs, and bobs, and other ways which I will not name, for the honor I bear them, so without measure misordered, that I think myself in hell, till time come that I must go to Mr. Elmer; who teacheth me so gently, so pleasantly, with such fair allurements to learning, that I think all the time nothing whiles I am with him. And when I am called from him, I fall on weeping, because whatsoever I do else but learning, is full of grief, trouble, fear, and whole misliking unto me. And thus my book hath been so much my pleasure, and bringeth daily to me more pleasure and more, that in respect of it, all other pleasures, in very deed, be but trifles and troubles unto me.''

I remember this talk gladly, both because it is so worthy of memory, and because also it was the last talk that ever I had, and the last time that ever I saw that noble and worthy lady.

JOHN FOXE

Born in 1516, died in 1587; educated at Oxford; became in 1584 tutor to the children of Henry Howard, Earl of Surrey; in order to escape persecution as a Protestant, fled to the Continent at the accession of Mary Tudor; returned to England in 1559, becoming in 1563 prebendary in Salisbury Cathedral; his "Book of Martyrs" first published in 1563.

THE DEATH OF ANNE BOLEYN [1]

In certain records thus we find, that the king, being in his justs at Greenwich, suddenly, with a few persons, departed to Westminster; and the next day after, Queen Anne, his wife, was had to the Tower, with the Lord Rochford, her brother, and certain other, and the nineteenth day after, was beheaded. The words of this worthy and Christian lady, at her death, were these: "Good Christian people, I am come hither to die; for, according to the law, and by the law, I am judged to death, and therefore I will speak nothing against it. I am come hither to accuse no man, nor to speak anything of that whereof I am accused, and condemned to die; but I pray God save the king, and send him long to reign over you, for a gentler or a more merciful prince was there never; and to me he was a very good, a gentle, and a sovereign lord. And if any person will meddle of my cause, I require them to

[1] From the "Book of Martyrs."

touching the memorable virtues of this worthy queen, partly we have said something before, partly because more also is promised to be declared of her virtuous life (the Lord so permitting), by other who then were about her, I will cease in this matter further to proceed.

SIR WALTER RALEIGH

Born in 1552, died in 1618; educated at Oxford; commanded an English Company in Ireland in 1580; a favorite
of Queen Elizabeth; obtained a charter to colonize Virginia
in 1584, and sent out several expeditions, none of which
founded permanent settlements; introduced tobacco into
Europe, and the potato into Ireland; took an active part
against the Armada in 1588; explored the Oronoko in 1595;
charged with having plotted to place Arabella Stuart on
the throne in 1603, and sent to the Tower, where he wrote
his "History of the World"; sailed again for the Oronoko
in 1616; and on his return, the expedition having failed,
condemned and executed.

THE MUTABILITY OF HUMAN AFFAIRS[1]

If we truly examine the difference of both conditions—to wit, of the rich and mighty, whom we
call fortunate, and of the poor and opprest, whom
we count wretched—we shall find the happiness
of the one, and the miserable estate of the other,
so tied by God to the very instant, and both so
subject to interchange (witness the sudden down-
fall of the greatest princes, and the speedy up-
rising of the meanest persons), as the one hath
nothing so certain whereof to boast, nor the other
so uncertain whereof to bewail itself.

For there is no man so assured of his honor, of
his riches, health, or life but that he may be
deprived of either, or all, the very next hour
or day to come. *Quid vesper vehat, incertum est;*
what the evening will bring with it is uncertain.

---

[1] From the preface to the "History of the World."

And yet ye can not tell, saith St. James, what shall be to-morrow. To-day he is set up, and to-morrow he shall not be found, for he is turned into dust, and his purpose perisheth. And altho the air which compasseth adversity be very obscure, yet therein we better discern God than in that shining light which environeth worldly glory; through which, for the clearness thereof, there is no vanity which escapeth our sight. And let adversity seem what it will—to happy men, ridiculous, who make themselves merry at other men's misfortunes; and to those under the cross, grievous—yet this is true, that for all that is past, to the very instant, the portions remaining are equal to either. For, be it that we have lived many years (according to Solomon), "and in them all we have rejoiced"; or be it that we have measured the same length of days, and therein have evermore sorrowed; yet, looking back from our present being, we find both the one and the other—to wit, the joy and the wo—sailed out of sight; and death, which doth pursue us and hold us in chase from our infancy, hath gathered it. *Quicquid ætatis retro est, mors tenet;* whatsoever of our age is past, death holds it.

So as, whosoever he be to whom fortune hath been a servant, and the time a friend, let him but take the account of his memory (for we have no other keeper of our pleasures past), and truly examine what it hath reserved, either of beauty and youth, or foregone delights; what it hath saved, that it might last, of his dearest affections, or of whatever else the amorous springtime gave his thoughts of contentment, then invaluable, and he shall find that all the art which his elder

years have can draw no other vapor out of these
dissolutions than heavy, secret, and sad sighs.
He shall find nothing remaining but those sor-
rows which grow up after our fast-springing
youth, overtake it when it is at a stand, and
overtop it utterly when it begins to wither; insomuch as, looking back from the very instant
time, and from our now being, the poor, diseased,
and captive creature hath as little sense of all
his former miseries and pains as he that is most
blest, in common opinion, hath of his forepast
pleasures and delights. For whatsoever is cast
behind us is just nothing; and what is to come,
deceitful hope hath it. *Omniæ quæ eventura sunt
in incerto jacent.* Only those few black swans
I must except who, having had the grace to value
worldly vanities at no more than their own price,
do, by retaining the comfortable memory of a
well-acted life, behold death without dread, and
the grave without fear, and embrace both as
necessary guides to endless glory. . . .

If we seek a reason of the succession and con-
tinuance of boundless ambition in mortal men,
we may add, that the kings and princes of the
world have always laid before them the actions,
but not the ends of those great ones which preceded them. They are always transported with
the glory of the one, but they never mind the
misery of the other, till they find the experience
in themselves. They neglect the advice of God
while they enjoy life, or hope it, but they follow
the counsel of death upon his first approach.
It is he that puts into man all the wisdom of
the world without speaking a word, which God,
with all the words of His law, promises, or

threats, doth not infuse. Death, which hateth and destroyeth man, is believed; God, which hath made him and loves him, is always deferred. "I have considered," saith Solomon, "all the works that are under the sun, and, behold, all is vanity and vexation of spirit"; but who believes it, till death tells it us? It was death, which, opening the conscience of Charles V. made him enjoin his son Philip to restore Navarre, and King Francis I. of France to command that justice should be done upon the murderers of the Protestants in Merindol and Cabrieres, which till then he neglected.

It is therefore death alone that can suddenly make man to know himself. He tells the proud and insolent that they are but abjects, and humbles them at the instant, makes them cry, complain, and repent, yea, even to hate their forepassed happiness. He takes the account of the rich, and proves him a beggar, a naked beggar, which hath interest in nothing but in the gravel that fills his mouth. He holds a glass before the eyes of the most beautiful, and makes them see therein their deformity and rottenness, and they acknowledge it.

O eloquent, just, and mighty Death! whom none could advise, thou hast persuaded; what none hath dared, thou hast done; and whom all the world hath flattered, thou only hast cast out of the world and despised; thou hast drawn together all the far-stretched greatness, all the pride, cruelty, and ambition of man, and covered it all over with these two narrow words, *Hic jacet!*

FRANCIS BACON

Born in 1561, died in 1626; commonly styled "Lord" Bacon, but incorrectly, his title being Baron Verulam and Viscount St. Albans; educated at Cambridge; entered Parliament in 1584; solicitor-general in 1607; privy counsellor in 1616; lord keeper in 1617; lord chancellor in 1618; tried for bribery, condemned, fined and removed from office in 1621; one of the chief founders of modern inductive science; author of "Advancement of Learning" (1605), the "Novum Organum" (1620), "Essays" (1597-1625), a "History of Henry VII" (1622) and other works.

I

OF TRAVEL[1]

TRAVEL, in the younger sort, is a part of education, in the elder, a part of experience. He that traveleth into a country before he hath some entrance into the language, goeth to school, and not to travel. That young men travel under some tutor, or grave servant, I allow well; so that he be such a one that hath the language, and hath been in the country before; whereby he may be able to tell them what things are worthy to be seen in the country where they go; what acquaintances they are to seek; what exercises or discipline the place yieldeth. For else young men shall go hooded, and look abroad little. It is a strange thing, that in sea voyages, where there is nothing to be seen but sky and sea, men should make diaries; but in land-travel, wherein so much is to be observed, for the most part they omit it; as if chance were fitter to be

[1] The selections here given from Bacon are all from the "Essays."

registered than observation. Let diaries therefore be brought in use. The things to be seen and observed are: the courts of princes, specially when they give audience to ambassadors; the courts of justice, while they sit and hear causes; and so of consistories ecclesiastic; the churches and monasteries, with the monuments which are therein extant; the walls and fortifications of cities and towns, and so the havens and harbors; antiquities and ruins; libraries, colleges, disputations, and lectures, where any are; shipping and navies; houses and gardens of state and pleasure, near great cities; armories; arsenals; magazines; exchanges; burses; warehouses; exercises of horsemanship, fencing, training of soldiers, and the like; comedies, such whereunto the better sort of persons do resort; treasuries of jewels and robes; cabinets and rarities; and, to conclude, whatsoever is memorable in the places where they go. After all which the tutors or servants ought to make diligent study. As for triumphs, masks, feasts, weddings, funerals, capital executions, and such shows, men need not to be put in mind of them; yet are they not to be neglected.

If you will have a young man to put his travel into a little room, and in short time to gather much, this you must do. First, as was said, he must have some entrance into the language before he goeth. Then he must have such a servant or tutor as knoweth the country, as was likewise said. Let him carry with him also some card or book describing the country where he traveleth; which will be a good key to his inquiry. Let him keep also a diary. Let him not stay long in one city or town; more or less as the place

deserveth, but not long; nay, when he stayeth
in one city or town, let him change his lodging
from one end and part of the town to another;
which is a great adamant of acquaintance. Let
him sequester himself from the company of his
countrymen, and diet in such places where there
is good company of the nation where he traveleth. Let him, upon his removes from one place
to another, procure recommendation to some person of quality residing in the place whither he
removeth; that he may use his favor in those
things he desireth to see or know. Thus he may
abridge his travel with much profit.

As for the acquaintance which is to be sought in
travel; that which is most of all profitable is
acquaintance with the secretaries and employed
men of ambassadors: for so in traveling in one
country he shall suck the experience of many.
Let him also see and visit eminent persons in
all kinds, which are of great name abroad; that
he may be able to tell how the life agreeth with
the fame. For quarrels, they are with care and
discretion to be avoided. They are commonly
for mistresses, healths, place, and words. And
let a man beware how he keepeth company with
choleric and quarrelsome persons; for they will
engage him into their own quarrels. When a
traveler returneth home, let him not leave the
countries where he hath traveled altogether behind him; but maintain a correspondence by letters with those of his acquaintance which are of
most worth. And let his travel appear rather in
his discourse than in his apparel or gesture; and
in his discourse let him be rather advised in his
answers, than forwards to tell stories; and let

it appear that he doth not change his country manners for those of foreign parts; but only prick in some flowers of that he hath learned abroad into the customs of his own country.

II

OF RICHES

I CANNOT call riches better than the baggage of virtue. The Roman word is better, *impedimenta.* For as the baggage is to an army, so is riches to virtue. It cannot be spared nor left behind, but it hindereth the march; yea, and the care of it sometimes loseth or disturbeth the victory. Of great riches there is no real use, except it be in the distribution; the rest is but conceit. So saith Solomon, "Where much is, there are many to consume it; and what hath the owner but the sight of it with his eyes?" The personal fruition in any man cannot reach to feel great riches: there is a custody of them; or a power of dole and donative of them; or a fame of them; but no solid use to the owner. Do you not see what feigned prices are set upon little stones and rarities? and what works of ostentation are undertaken, because there might seem to be some use of great riches? But then you will say, they may be of use to buy men out of dangers or troubles. As Solomon saith, "Riches are as a stronghold, in the imagination of the rich man."

But this is excellently exprest, that it is in imagination, and not always in fact. For certainly great riches have sold more men than they have bought out. Seek not proud riches, but such as thou mayest get justly, use soberly, distribute cheerfully, and leave contentedly. Yet have no abstract or friarly contempt of them. But distinguish as Cicero saith well of Rabirius Posthumus, *In studio rei amplificandæ apparebat, non avaritiæ prædam, sed instrumentum bonitari quæri.*[1] Harken also to Solomon, and beware of hasty gathering of riches: *Qui festinat ad divitias, non erit insons.*[2] The poets feign, that when Plutus (which is Riches) is sent from Jupiter, he limps and goes slowly; but when he is sent from Pluto, he runs and is swift of foot. Meaning that riches gotten by good means and just labor pace slowly; but when they come by the death of others (as by the course of inheritance, testaments, and the like), they come tumbling upon a man. But it might be applied likewise to Pluto, taking him for the devil. For when riches come from the devil (as by fraud and oppression and unjust means), they come upon speed.

The ways to enrich are many, and most of them foul. Parsimony is one of the best, and yet is not innocent; for it withholdeth men from works of liberality and charity. The improvement of the ground is the most natural obtaining of riches; for it is our great mother's blessing, the earth's; but it is slow. And yet where men of great wealth do stoop to husbandry, it multi-

---

[1] Cicero's meaning is that Rabirius was not prompted by avarice so much as by a desire to obtain the means whereby he could do good.

[2] This has commonly been translated as "He that maketh haste to become rich shall not remain innocent."

plieth riches exceedingly. I knew a nobleman in England, that had the greatest audits of any man in my time; a great grazier, a great sheepmaster, a great timber man, a great collier, a great corn-master, a great lead-man, and so of iron, and a number of the like points of husbandry. So as the earth seemed a sea to him, n respect of the perpetual importation. It was truly observed by one, that himself came very hardly to a little riches, and very easily to great riches. For when a man's stock is come to that, that he can expect the prime of markets, and overcome those bargains which for their greatness are few men's money, and be partner in the industries of younger men, he cannot but increase mainly.

The gains of ordinary trades and vocations are honest; and furthered by two things chiefly: by diligence, and by a good name for good and fair dealing. But the gains of bargains are of a more doubtful nature; when men shall wait upon others' necessity, broke by servants and instruments to draw them on, put off others cunningly that would be better chapmen, and the like practises, which are crafty and naught. As for the chopping of bargains, when a man buys not to hold but to sell over again, that commonly grindeth double, both upon the seller and upon the buyer. Sharings do greatly enrich, if the hands be well chosen that are trusted. Usury is the certainest means of gain, tho one of the worst; as that whereby a man doth eat his bread *in sudore vultus alieni;*[3] and besides, doth

---

[3] The meaning is in the sweat of another man's brow rather than one's own.

plough upon Sundays. But yet certain tho it be, it hath flaws; for that the scriveners and brokers do value unsound men to serve their own turn. The fortune in being the first in an invention or in a privilege doth cause sometimes a wonderful overgrowth in riches; as it was with the first sugar man in the Canaries.[4] Therefore if a man can play the true logician, to have as well judgment as invention, he may do great matters; especially if the times be fit.

He that resteth upon gains certain shall hardly grow to great riches; and he that puts all upon adventures doth oftentimes break and come to poverty: it is good therefore to guard adventures with certainties, that may uphold losses. Monopolies, and co-emption of wares for re-sale, where they are not restrained, are great means to enrich; especially if the party have intelligence what things are like to come into request, and so store himself beforehand. Riches gotten by service, tho it be of the best rise, yet when they are gotten by flattery, feeding humors, and other servile conditions, they may be placed amongst the worst. As for fishing for testaments and executorships (as Tacitus saith of Seneca, *testamenta et orbos tamquam indagine capi*,[5]) it is yet worse; by how much men submit themselves to meaner persons than in service. Believe not much them that seem to despise riches; for they

[4] Sugar is one of the chief products of the Canary Islands. These islands are supposed to be identical with those known to the ancients as the Fortunate Islands.

[5] The remark of Tacitus means that Seneca took profitable places of trust in such numbers that it was as if he had gathered them in with a net.

despise them that despair of them; and none worse when they come to them. Be not penny-wise; riches have wings, and sometimes they fly away of themselves, sometimes they must be set flying to bring in more. Men leave their riches either to their kindred, or to the public; and moderate portions prosper best in both. A great estate left to an heir, is as a lure to all the birds of prey round about to seize on him, if he be not the better established in years and judgment. Likewise glorious gifts and foundations are like sacrifices without salt; and but the painted sepulchers of alms, which soon will putrefy and corrupt inwardly. Therefore measure not thine advancements by quantity, but frame them by measure: and defer not charities till death; for, certainly, if a man weigh it rightly, he that doth so is rather liberal of another man's than of his own.

III

OF YOUTH AND AGE

A MAN that is young in years may be old in hours, if he have lost no time. But that happeneth rarely. Generally, youth is like the first cogitations, not so wise as the second. For there is a youth in thoughts, as well as in ages. And yet the invention of young men is more lively than that of old; and imaginations stream into their minds better, and as it were more divinely. Natures that have much heat and great and violent desires and perturbations are not ripe for action till they have passed the meridian of their years; as it was with Julius Cæsar and Septimius Severus. Of the latter of whom it is said, *Juventutem egit erroribus, imo furoribus, plenam.*[6] And yet he was the ablest emperor, almost, of all the list. But reposed natures may do well in youth. As it is seen in Augustus Cæsar, Cosmus Duke of Florence, Gaston de Foix, and others. On the other side, heat and vivacity in age is an excellent composition for business.

Young men are fitter to invent than to judge; fitter for execution than for counsel; and fitter for new projects than for settled business. For the experience of age, in things that fall within the compass of it, directeth them; but in new things, abuseth them. The errors of young men are the ruin of business; but the errors of aged men amount but to this, that more might have been done, or sooner. Young men, in the conduct and manage of actions, embrace more than they can hold; stir more than they can quiet; fly to the end, without consideration of the means and degrees; pursue some few principles which they have chanced upon absurdly; care not to innovate, which draws unknown inconveniences; use extreme remedies at first; and that which doubleth all errors will not acknowledge or retract them; like an unready horse, that will neither stop nor turn. Men of age object too much, consult too long, adventure too little, repent too soon, and seldom drive business home to the full

[6] The meaning is that Severus passed his youth, not only in errors, but that his youth was so full of them as to have been almost one of madness.

period, but content themselves with a mediocrity.

Certainly it is good to compound employments of both; for that will be good for the present, because the virtues of either age may correct the defects of both; and good for succession, that young men may be learners, while men in age are actors; and, lastly, good for extern accidents, because authority followeth old men, and favor and popularity youth. But for the moral part, perhaps youth will have the preeminence, as age hath for the politic. A certain rabbin, upon the text, *Your young men shall see visions, and your old men shall dream dreams*, inferreth that young men are admitted nearer to God than old, because vision is a clearer revelation than a dream. And certainly, the more a man drinketh of the world, the more it intoxicateth; and age doth profit rather in the powers of understanding, than in the virtues of the will and affections. There be some have an over-early ripeness in their years, which fadeth betimes. These are, first, such as have brittle wits, the edge whereof is soon turned; such as was Hermogenes[7] the rhetorician, whose books are exceeding subtle; who afterwards waxed stupid.

A second sort is of those that have some natural dispositions which find better grace in youth than in age; such as is a fluent and luxuriant speech; which becomes youth well, but not age: so Tully saith of Hortensius,[8] *Idem manebat,*

[7] Hermogenes, a native of Tarsus, lived in the second century A.D.

[8] Hortensius was a Roman orator of Cicero's time and an early rival of his. The remark here quoted from Tully (Cicero) means that Hortensius continued a line of action until it was not becoming.

neque idem decebat. The third is of such as take
too high a strain at the first, and are magnanimous more than tract of years can uphold. As
was Scipio Africanus, of whom Livy saith* in
effect, *Ultima primis cedebant.*

IV

OF REVENGE

REVENGE is a kind of wild justice; which the
more man's nature runs to, the more ought law
to weed it out. For as for the first wrong, it
doth but offend the law; but the revenge of that
wrong putteth the law out of office. Certainly, in
taking revenge, a man is but even with his enemy; but in passing it over, he is superior; for
it is a prince's part to pardon. And Solomon,
I am sure, saith, *It is the glory of a man to pass
by an offense.* That which is past is gone, and
irrevocable; and wise men have enough to do
with things present and to come; therefore they
do but trifle with themselves, that labor in past
matters. There is no man doth a wrong for the
wrong's sake; but thereby to purchase himself
profit, or pleasure, or honor, or the like. Therefore why should I be angry with a man for loving
himself better than me? And if any man should
do wrong merely out of ill-nature, why, yet it
is but like the thorn or brier, which prick and
scratch, because they can do no other.

* Livy's remark means that Scipio in old age was not equal
to himself in his youth in the things he performed.

The most tolerable sort of revenge is for those wrongs which there is no law to remedy; but then let a man take heed the revenge be such as there is no law to punish; else a man's enemy is still beforehand, and it is two for one. Some, when they take revenge, are desirous the party should know whence it cometh. This is the more generous. For the delight seemeth to be not so much in doing the hurt as in making the party repent. But base and crafty cowards are like the arrow that flieth in the dark. Cosmus,[10] Duke of Florence, had a desperate saying against perfidious or neglecting friends, as if those wrongs were unpardonable: *You shall read* (saith he) *that we are commanded to forgive our enemies; but you never read that we are commanded to forgive our friends.* But yet the spirit of Job was in a better tune: *Shall we* (saith he) *take good at God's hands, and not be content to take evil also?* And so of friends in a proportion. This is certain, that a man that studieth revenge keeps his own wounds green, which otherwise would heal and do well. Public revenges are for the most part fortunate; as that for the death of Cæsar; for the death of Pertinax;[11] for the death of Henry the Third of France;[12] and many more. But in private revenges it is not so. Nay rather, vindictive persons live the life of witches; who, as they are mischievous, so end they infortunate.

[10] Now written Cosmo, or Cosimo. He became duke in 1537.

[11] Pertinax, the Roman emperor, was murdered by the Pretorian Guards in 193 A.D. The guards were put to death by order of Septimius Severus, his successor.

[12] Henry was murdered by a monk named Clement, who was put to death for the crime.

V

OF MARRIAGE AND SINGLE LIFE

HE that hath wife and children hath given hostages to fortune; for they are impediments to great enterprises, either of virtue or mischief. Certainly the best works, and of greatest merit for the public, have proceeded from the unmarried or childless men; which both in affection and means have married and endowed the public. Yet it were great reason that those that have children should have greatest care of future times; unto which they know they must transmit their dearest pledges. Some there are, who tho they lead a single life, yet their thoughts do end with themselves, and account future times impertinences. Nay, there are some other that account wife and children but as bills of charges. Nay more, there are some foolish rich covetous men, that take a pride in having no children, because they may be thought so much the richer. For perhaps they have heard some talk, *Such an one is a great rich man*, and another except to it, *Yea, but he hath a great charge of children;* as if it were an abatement to his riches.

But the most ordinary cause of a single life is liberty, especially in certain self-pleasing and humorous minds, which are so sensible of every restraint, as they will go near to think their girdles and garters to be bonds and shackles. Unmarried men are best friends, best masters, best servants; but not always best subjects; for they are light to run away; and almost all fugitives are of that condition. A single life doth well with churchmen; for charity will hardly water the ground where it must first fill a pool. It is indifferent for judges and magistrates; for if they be facile and corrupt, you shall have a servant five times worse than a wife. For soldiers, I find the generals commonly in their hortatives put men in mind of their wives and children; and I think the despising of marriage among the Turks maketh the vulgar soldier more base.

Certainly wife and children are a kind of discipline of humanity; and single men, tho they may be many times more charitable, because their means are less exhaust, yet, on the other side, they are more cruel and hard-hearted (good to make severe inquisitors), because their tenderness is not so oft called upon.

Grave natures, led by custom, and therefore constant, are commonly loving husbands, as was said of Ulysses,[13] *vetulam suam prætulit immortalitati.* Chaste women are often proud and froward, as presuming upon the merit of their chastity. It is one of the best bonds both of chastity and obedience in the wife, if she think her husband wise; which she will never do if she find him jealous. Wives are young men's mistresses; companions for middle age; and old men's nurses. So as a man may have a quarrel to marry when he will. But yet he was reputed one of the wise men, that made answer to the question, when a man should marry—*A young man not yet, an elder man not at all.* It is often

---

[13] This refers to the refusal of Ulysses to wed a goddess, preferring his own wife, who was no longer young.

seen that bad husbands have very good wives;
whether it be that it raiseth the price of their
husband's kindness when it comes; or that the
wives take a pride in their patience. But this
never fails, if the bad husbands were of their
own choosing, against their friends' consent; for
then they will be sure to make good their own
folly.

VI

OF ENVY

THERE be none of the affections which have
been noted to fascinate or bewitch, but love and
envy. They both have vehement wishes; they
frame themselves readily into imaginations and
suggestions; and they come easily into the eye,
especially upon the presence of the objects;
which are the points that conduce to fascination,
if any such thing there be. We see likewise the
Scripture calleth envy an evil eye; and the as-
trologers call the evil influences of the stars evil
aspects; so that still there seemeth to be ac-
knowledged, in the act of envy, an ejaculation
or irradiation of the eye. Nay some have been
so curious as to note that the times when the
stroke or percussion of an envious eye doth most
hurt are when the party envied is beheld in glory
or triumph; for that sets an edge upon envy:
and besides, at such times the spirits of the person envied do come forth most into the outward
parts, and so meet the blow.

But leaving these curiosities (tho not unworthy to be thought on in fit place), we will handle, what persons are apt to envy others; what persons are most subject to be envied themselves; and what is the difference between public and private envy.

A man that hath no virtue in himself, ever envieth virtue in others. For men's minds will either feed upon their own good or upon others' evil; and who wanteth the one will prey upon the other; and whoso is out of hope to attain to another's virtue, will seek to come at even hand by depressing another's fortune.

A man that is busy and inquisitive is commonly envious. For to know much of other men's matters cannot be because all that ado may concern his own estate; therefore it must needs be that he taketh a kind of play-pleasure in looking upon the fortunes of others. Neither can he that mindeth but his own business find much matter for envy. For envy is a gadding passion, and walketh the streets, and doth not keep home: *Non est curiosus, quin idem sit malevolus.* [14]

Men of noble birth are noted to be envious towards new men when they rise. For the distance is altered; and it is like a deceit of the eye, that when others come on they think themselves go back.

Deformed persons, and eunuchs, and old men, and bastards, are envious. For he that can not possibly mend his own case will do what he can to impair another's; except these defects light

[14] The meaning is that no man is possest by curiosity unless some malevolence inspires him.

upon a very brave and heroical nature, which thinketh to make his natural wants part of his honor; in that it should be said, that an eunuch, or a lame man, did such great matters; affecting the honor of a miracle; as it was in Narses[15] the eunuch, and Agesilaus[16] and Tamberlanes,[17] that were lame men.

The same is the case of men that rise after calamities and misfortunes. For they are as men fallen out with the times; and think other men's harms a redemption of their own sufferings.

They that desire to excel in too many matters, out of levity and vainglory, are ever envious. For they can not want work; it being impossible but many in some one of those things should surpass them. Which was the character of Adrian[18] the Emperor; that mortally envied poets and painters and artificers, in works wherein he had a vein to excel.

Lastly, near kinsfolks, and fellows in office, and those that have been bred together, are more apt to envy their equals when they are raised. For it doth upbraid unto them their own fortunes, and pointeth at them, and cometh oftener into their remembrance, and incurreth likewise more into the note of others; and envy ever redoubleth from speech and fame. Cain's envy

[15] Narses was the associate of Belisarius in command of the Roman army in Italy in 538-539, and greatly distinguished himself as the sole commander in later years.

[16] Agesilaus was a famous king of Sparta.

[17] Now commonly written Tamerlane, which stands for Timour the Lame, Timour being his real name.

[18] Adrian, now commonly called Hadrian, emperor of Rome, was born in 76, and died in 138.

was the more vile and malignant towards his brother Abel, because when his sacrifice was better accepted there was no body to look on. Thus much for those that are apt to envy.

Concerning those that are more or less subject to envy: First, persons of eminent virtue, when they are advanced, are less envied. For their fortune seemeth but due unto them; and no man envieth the payment of a debt, but rewards and liberality rather. Again, envy is ever joined with the comparing of a man's self; and where there is no comparison, no envy; and therefore kings are not envied but by kings. Nevertheless it is to be noted that unworthy persons are most envied at their first coming in, and afterwards overcome it better; whereas contrariwise, persons of worth and merit are most envied when their fortune continueth long. For by that time, tho their virtue be the same, yet it hath not the same luster; for fresh men grow up that darken it.

Persons of noble blood are less envied in their rising. For it seemeth but right done to their birth. Besides, there seemeth not much added to their fortune; and envy is as the sunbeams, that beat hotter upon a bank or steep rising ground, than up a flat. And for the same reason those that are advanced by degrees are less envied than those that are advanced suddenly and *per saltum* [at a bound].

Those that have joined with their honor great travels, cares, or perils, are less subject to envy. For men think that they earn their honors hardly, and pity them sometimes; and pity ever healeth envy. Wherefore you shall observe that the more deep and sober sort of politic persons, in their greatness, are ever bemoaning themselves, what a life they lead; chanting a *quanta patimur*. Not that they feel it so, but only to abate the edge of envy. But this is to be understood of business that is laid upon men, and not such as they call unto themselves. For nothing increaseth envy more than an unnecessary and ambitious engrossing of business. And nothing doth extinguish envy more than for a great person to preserve all other inferior officers in their full rights and preeminences of their places. For by that means there be so many screens between him and envy.

Above all, those are most subject to envy, which carry the greatness of their fortunes in an insolent and proud manner; being never well but while they are showing how great they are, either by outward pomp, or by triumphing over all opposition or competition; whereas wise men will rather do sacrifice to envy, in suffering themselves sometimes of purpose to be crossed and overborne in things that do not much concern them. Notwithstanding, so much is true, that the carriage of greatness in a plain and open manner (so it be without arrogancy and vain glory) doth draw less envy than if it be in a more crafty and cunning fashion. For in that course a man doth but disavow fortune; and seemeth to be conscious of his own want in worth; and doth but teach others to envy him.

Lastly, to conclude this part; as we said in the beginning that the act of envy had somewhat in it of witchcraft, so there is no other cure of envy but the cure of witchcraft; and that is, to remove the *lot* (as they call it) and to lay it upon another. For which purpose, the wiser sort of great persons bring in ever upon the stage somebody upon whom to derive the envy that would come upon themselves; sometimes upon ministers and servants; sometimes upon colleagues and associates; and the like; and for that turn there are never wanting some persons of violent and undertaking nature, who, so they may have power and business, will take it at any cost.

Now, to speak of public envy. There is yet some good in public envy, whereas in private there is none. For public envy is as an ostracism, that eclipseth men when they grow too great. And therefore it is a bridle also to great ones, to keep them within bounds.

This envy, being in the Latin word *invidia*, goeth in the modern languages by the name of *discontentment;* of which we shall speak in handling sedition. It is a disease in a state like to infection. For as infection spreadeth upon that which is sound, and tainteth it; so when envy is gotten once into a state, it traduceth even the best actions thereof, and turneth them into an ill odor. And therefore there is little won by intermingling of plausible actions. For that doth argue but a weakness and fear of envy, which hurteth so much the more, as it is likewise usual in infections; which if you fear them, you call them upon you.

This public envy seemeth to beat chiefly upon principal officers or ministers, rather than upon kings and estates themselves. But this is a sure rule, that if the envy upon the minister be great, when the cause of it in him is small; or if the envy be general in a manner upon all the ministers of an estate; then the envy (tho hidden) is truly upon the state itself. And so much of public envy or discontentment, and the difference thereof from private envy, which was handled in the first place.

We will add this in general, touching the affection of envy; that of all other affections it is the most importune and continual. For of other affections there is occasion given but now and then; and therefore it was well said, *Invidia festos dies non agit:*[19] for it is ever working upon some or other. And it is also noted that love and envy do make a man pine, which other affections do not, because they are not so continual. It is also the vilest affection, and the most depraved; for which cause it is the proper attribute of the devil, who is called *the envious man, that soweth tares amongst the wheat by night;* as it always cometh to pass, that envy worketh subtilly, and in the dark; and to the prejudice of good things, such as is the wheat.

[19] This saying has been translated "Envy keeps no holidays."

Neither is there only a habit of goodness, directed by right reason; but there is in some men, even in nature, a disposition towards it; as on the other side there is a natural malignity. For there be that in their nature do not affect the good of others. The lighter sort of malignity turneth but to a crossness, or frowardness, or aptness to oppose, or difficilness, or the like; but the deeper sort to envy and mere mischief. Such men in other men's calamities are, as it were, in season, and are ever on the loading part: not so good as the dogs that licked Lazarus' sores; but like flies that are still buzzing upon anything that is raw; *misanthropi* [haters of men], that make it their practise to bring men to the bough, and yet have never a tree for the purpose in their gardens, as Timon [23] had. Such dispositions are the very errors of human nature; and yet they are the fittest timber to make great politics of; like to knee timber, that is good for ships, that are ordained to be tossed; but not for building houses, that shall stand firm. The parts and signs of goodness are many. If a man be gracious and courteous to strangers, it shows he is a citizen of the world, and that his heart is no island cut off from other lands, but a continent that joins to them. If he be compassionate towards the afflictions of others, it shows that his heart is like the noble tree that is wounded itself when it gives the balm. If he easily pardons and remits offenses, it shows that his mind is planted above injuries; so that he cannot be shot. If he be thankful for small

[23] The reference is to Timon of Athens, a real person, who is the subject of one of Shakespeare's plays.

benefits, it shows that he weighs men's minds, and not their trash. But above all, if he have St. Paul's perfection, that he would wish to be an *anathema* from Christ for the salvation of his brethren, it shows much of a divine nature, and a kind of conformity with Christ Himself.

VIII

OF STUDIES

STUDIES serve for delight, for ornament, and for ability. Their chief use for delight is in privateness and retiring; for ornament is in discourse; and for ability is in the judgment and disposition of business. For expert men can execute, and perhaps judge of particulars, one by one; but the general counsels, and the plots and marshaling of affairs, come best from those that are learned. To spend too much time in studies is sloth; to use them too much for ornament, is affectation; to make judgment wholly by their rules, is the humor of a scholar. They perfect nature, and are perfected by experience: for natural abilities are like natural plants, that need proyning,[24] by study; and studies themselves do give forth directions too much at large, except they be bounded in by experience. Crafty men contemn studies, simple men admire them, and wise men use them; for they teach not their own

[24] An early form of the word pruning, which once had a wider meaning than now.

use; but that is a wisdom without them, and above them, won by observation. Read not to contradict and confute; nor to believe and take for granted; nor to find talk and discourse; but to weigh and consider. Some books are to be tasted, others to be swallowed, and some few to be chewed and digested; that is, some books are to be read only in parts; others to be read, but not curiously; and some few to be read wholly, and with diligence and attention. Some books also may be read by deputy, and extracts made of them by others; but that would be only in the less important arguments, and the meaner sort of books; else distilled books are like common distilled waters, flashy things. Reading maketh a full man; conference a ready man; and writing an exact man.

And therefore, if a man write little, he had need have a great memory; if he confer little, he had need have a present wit: and if he read little, he had need have much cunning, to seem to know that he doth not. Histories make men wise; poets witty; the mathematics subtile; natural philosophy deep; moral grave; logic and rhetoric able to contend. *Abeunt studia in mores.*[25] Nay, there is no stond or impediment in the wit but may be wrought out by fit studies; like as diseases of the body may have appropriate exercises. Bowling is good for the stone and reins; shooting for the lungs and breast; gentle walking for the stomach; riding for the head; and the like. So if a man's wit be wandering, let him study the mathematics; for in demonstrations,

[25] The meaning is that manners are deeply influenced by one's studies.

if his wit be called away never so little, he must begin again. If his wit be not apt to distinguish or find differences, let him study the Schoolmen; for they are *cymini sectores* [splitters of hairs]. If he be not apt to beat over matters, and to call up one thing to prove and illustrate another, let him study the lawyers' cases. So every defect of the mind may have a special receipt.

IX

OF REGIMENT OF HEALTH

THERE is a wisdom in this beyond the rules of physic: a man's own observation, what he finds good of, and what he finds hurt of, is the best physic to preserve health. But it is a safer conclusion to say, *This agreeth not well with me, therefore I will not continue it;* than this, *I find no offense of this, therefore I may use it.* For strength of nature in youth passeth over many excesses, which are owing a man till his age. Discern of the coming on of years, and think not to do the same things still; for age will not be defied. Beware of sudden change in any great point of diet, and if necessity inforce it, fit the rest to it. For it is a secret in nature and state, that it is safer to change many things than one. Examine thy customs of diet, sleep, exercise, apparel, and the like; and try, in any thing thou shalt judge hurtful, to discontinue it by little and little; but so, as if thou dost find any inconvenience by the change, thou come back to it again: for it is hard to distinguish that which is generally held good and wholesome, from that which is good particularly, and fit for thine own body.

To be free-minded and cheerfully disposed at hours of meat and of sleep and of exercise, is one of the best precepts of long lasting. As for the passions and studies of the mind; avoid envy; anxious fears, anger fretting inwards; subtle and knotty inquisitions; joys and exhilarations in excess; sadness not communicated. Entertain hopes; mirth rather than joy; variety of delights, rather than surfeit of them; wonder and admiration, and therefore novelties; studies that fill the mind with splendid and illustrious objects, as histories, fables, and contemplations of nature. If you fly physic in health altogether, it will be too strange for your body when you shall need it. If you make it too familiar, it will work no extraordinary effect when sickness cometh. I commend rather some diet for certain seasons, than frequent use of physic, except it be grown into a custom. For those diets alter the body more, and trouble it less.

Despise no new accident in your body, but ask opinion of it. In sickness, respect health principally; and in health, action. For those that put their bodies to endure in health, may in most sicknesses, which are not very sharp, be cured only with diet and tendering. Celsus[26] could never have spoken it as a physician, had he not been a wise man withal, when he giveth it for

[26] Aulus Celsus, a Roman writer on medicine, who lived in the first half of the first century A.D.

one of the great precepts of health and lasting,
that a man do vary and interchange contraries,
but with an inclination to the more benign extreme: use fasting and full eating, but rather
full eating; watching and sleep, but rather sleep;
sitting and exercise, but rather exercise; and the
like.   So shall nature be cherished, and yet
taught masteries.   Physicians are some of them
so pleasing and conformable to the humor of the
patient, as they press not the true cure of the
disease; and some other are so regular in pro-
ceeding according to art for the disease, as they
respect not sufficiently the condition of the patient.   Take one of a middle temper; or if it
may not be found in one man, combine two of
either sort; and forget not to call as well the
best acquainted with your body, as the best
reputed of for his faculty.

SHAKESPEARE

Born in 1564; died in 1616; married Anne Hathaway in 1582; went to London and became an actor in 1587; began to revise, or write, plays in 1589; bought "New Place" at Stratford in 1597; retired from the theater in 1610; his plays first collected in the Folio of 1623.

I

BRUTUS TO HIS COUNTRYMEN[1]

Brutus. Be patient till the last.

Romans, countrymen, and lovers! hear me for my cause, and be silent, that you may hear; believe me for mine honor, and have respect to mine honor, that you may believe; censure me in your wisdom, and awake your senses, that you may the better judge. If there be any in this assembly, any dear friend of Cæsar's, to him I say, that Brutus' love to Cæsar was no less than his. If then that friend demand why Brutus rose against Cæsar, this is my answer: Not that I lov'd Cæsar less, but that I lov'd Rome more. Had you rather Cæsar were living and die all slaves, than that Cæsar were dead, to live all freemen? As Cæsar lov'd me, I weep for him; as he was fortunate, I rejoice at it; as he was valiant, I honor him; but as he was ambitious, I slew him. There is tears for his love; joy for his fortune; honor for his valor; and death for his ambition. Who is here so

[1] From "Julius Cæsar," Act III, Sc. ii.

base that would be a bondman? If any, speak;
for him have I offended. Who is here so rude
that would not be a Roman? If any, speak; for
him have I offended. Who is here so vile that
will not love his country? If any, speak; for
him have I offended. I pause for reply.

All. None, Brutus, none.

Brutus. Then none have I offended. I have
done no more to Cæsar than you shall do to
Brutus. The question of his death is enroll'd
in the Capitol; his glory not extenuated, wherein
he was worthy, nor his offenses enforc'd, for
which he suffered death.

—*Enter Antony (and others), with Cæsar's
body.*

Here comes his body, mourn'd by Mark Antony; who, tho he had no hand in his death,
shall receive the benefit of his dying, a place in
the commonwealth; as which of you shall not?
With this I depart, that, as I slew my best lover
for the good of Rome, I have the same dagger
for myself, when it shall please my country to
need my death.

II

SHYLOCK IN DEFENSE OF HIS RACE[1]

Shylock. There I have another bad match. A
bankrupt, a prodigal, who dare scarce show his
head on the Rialto; a beggar, that was us'd to
come so smug upon the mart; let him look to

[2] From "The Merchant of Venice," Act III, Sc. ii.

his bond. He was wont to call me usurer; let him look to his bond. He was wont to lend money for a Christian courtesy; let him look to his bond.

Salarino. Why, I am sure, if he forfeit, thou wilt not take his flesh. What's that good for?

Shylock. To bait fish withal. If it will feed nothing else, it will feed my revenge. He hath disgrac'd me, and hind'red me half a million; laugh'd at my losses, mock'd at my gains, scorned my nation, thwarted my bargains, cooled my friends, heated mine enemies; and what's his reason? I am a Jew. Hath not a Jew eyes? Hath not a Jew hands, organs, dimensions, senses, affections, passions; fed with the same food, hurt with the same weapons, subject to the same diseases, healed by the same means, warmed and cooled by the same winter and summer, as a Christian is? If you prick us, do we not bleed? If you tickle us, do we not laugh? If you poison us, do we not die? And if you wrong us, shall we not revenge? If we are like you in the rest, we will resemble you in that. If a Jew wrong a Christian, what is his humility? Revenge. If a Christian wrong a Jew, what should his sufferance be by Christian example? Why, revenge. The villainy you teach me, I will execute, and it shall go hard but I will better the instruction.

III

HAMLET TO THE PLAYERS [3]

Hamlet. Speak the speech, I pray you, as I pronounc'd it to you, trippingly on the tongue; but if you mouth it, as many of your players do, I had as lief the town-crier spoke my lines. Nor do not saw the air too much with your hand, thus, but use all gently; for in the very torrent, tempest, and, as I may say, the whirlwind of passion, you must acquire and beget a temperance that may give it smoothness. O, it offends me to the soul to see a robustious periwig-pated fellow tear a passion to tatters, to very rags, to split the ears of the groundlings, who for the most part are capable of nothing but inexplicable dumb-shows and noise. I could have such a fellow whipp'd for o'erdoing Termagant. It out-herods Herod. Pray you, avoid it.

First Player. I warrant your honor.

Hamlet. Be not too tame neither, but let your own discretion be your tutor. Suit the action to the word, the word to the action; with this special observance, that you o'erstep not the modesty of nature. For anything so overdone is from the purpose of playing, whose end, both at the first and now, was and is, to hold, as 'twere, the mirror up to nature; to show virtue her own feature, scorn her own image, and the very age and body of the time his form and pressure. Now this overdone, or come tardy

[3] From "Hamlet, Prince of Denmark," Act III, sc. ii.

off, tho it make the unskilful laugh, can not but make the judicious grieve; the censure of the which one must, in your allowance, o'erweigh a whole theater of others. O, there be players that I have seen play, and heard others praise, and that highly, not to speak it profanely, that, neither having the accent of Christians nor the gait of Christian, pagan, nor man, have so strutted and bellowed that I have thought some of Nature's journeymen had made men and not made them well, they imitated humanity so abominably.

First Player. I hope we have reform'd that indifferently with us, sir.

Hamlet. O, reform it altogether. And let those that play your clowns speak no more than is set down for them; for there be of them that will themselves laugh to set on some quantity of barren spectators to laugh too tho in the mean time some necessary question of the play be then to be considered. That's villainous, and shows a most pitiful ambition in the Fool that uses it. Go, make you ready.

[*Exeunt Players.*

BEN JONSON

Born in 1573; died in 1637; became a player in 1597;
his first play, "Everyman in His Humor," performed at the
Globe Theater in 1598, Shakespeare taking one of the parts;
went to France in 1613 as tutor to a son of Raleigh; visited
Drummond of Hawthornden in 1618; his library, one of
the finest in England, burned about 1621; his works first
collected in 1616; buried in Poet's Corner, Westminster,
Abbey.

OF SHAKESPEARE AND OTHER WITS [1]

I REMEMBER the players that have often mentioned it as an honor to Shakespeare, that in
his writing, whatsoever he penned, he never
blotted out a line. My answer hath been, "Would
he had blotted a thousand," which they thought
a malevolent speech. I had not told posterity
this, but for their ignorance who chose that
circumstance to commend their friend by wherein
he most faulted; and to justify mine own candor,
for I loved the man, and do honor his memory
on this side idolatry as much as any. He was,
indeed, honest, and of an open and free nature;
had an excellent phantasy, brave notions, and
gentle expressions, wherein he flowed with that
facility, that sometimes it was necessary he
should be stopt. *Sufflaminandus erat*, as Augustus said of Haterius. His wit was in his own
power: would the rule of it had been so too.
Many times he fell into those things which could

[1] From "Timber; or Discoveries Made upon Men and
Matter."

not escape laughter, as when he said in the person of Cæsar, one speaking to him, "Cæsar, thou dost me wrong." He replied, "Cæsar did never wrong but with just cause"; and such like, which were ridiculous. But he redeemed his vices with his virtues. There was ever more in him to be praised than to be pardoned.

In the difference of wits I have observed there are many notes; and it is a little maistry to know them, to discern what every nature, every disposition will bear; for before we sow our land we should plough it. There are no fewer forms of minds than of bodies amongst us. The variety is incredible, and therefore we must search. Some are fit to make divines, some poets, some lawyers, some physicians, some to be sent to the plow, and trades.

There is no doctrine will do good where nature is wanting. Some wits are swelling and high; others low and still; some hot and fiery; others cold and dull; one must have a bridle, the other a spur. There be some that are forward and bold; and these will do every little thing easily. I mean that is hard by and next them, which they will utter unretarded without any shame-facedness. These never perform much, but quickly. They are what they are on the sudden; they show presently like grain that, scattered on the top the ground, shoots up, but takes no root; has a yellow blade, but the ear empty. They are wits of good promise at first, but there is an *ingenistitium;* they stand still at sixteen, they get no higher. You have others that labor only to ostentation; and are ever more busy about the colors and surface of a work than in the matter and foundation, for that is hid, the other is seen.

Others that in composition are nothing but what is rough and broken. *Quæ per salebras, altaque saxa cadunt.* And if it would come gently, they trouble it of purpose. They would not have it run without rubs, as if that style were more strong and manly that struck the ear with a kind of unevenness. These men err not by chance, but knowingly and willingly; they are like men that affect a fashion by themselves; have some singularity in a ruff, cloak, or hatband; or their beards specially cut to provoke beholders, and set a mark upon themselves. They would be reprehended while they are looked on. And this vice, one that is authority with the rest, loving, delivers over to them to be imitated; so that ofttimes the faults which he fell into, the others seek for. This is the danger, when vice becomes a precedent.

Others there are that have no composition at all; but a kind of tuning and riming fall in what they write. It runs and slides, and only makes a sound. Women's poets they are called, as you have women's tailors.

> "They write a verse as smooth, as soft as
> cream,
> In which there is no torrent, nor scarce
> stream."

You may sound these wits and find the depth of them with your middle finger. They are creambowl, or but puddle-deep.

Some that turn over all books, and are equally searching in all papers; that write out of what they presently find or meet, without choice. By which means it happens that what they have discredited and impugned in one week, they have before or after extolled the same in another. Such are all the essayists, even their master Montaigne. These, in all they write, confess still what books they have read last, and therein their own folly so much that they bring it to the stake raw and undigested; not that the place did need it neither, but that they thought themselves furnished and would vent it. . . .

It cannot but come to pass that these men who commonly seek to do more than enough may sometimes happen on something that is good and great; but very seldom: and when it comes it doth not recompense the rest of their ill. For their jests, and their sentences (which they only and ambitiously seek for) stick out and are more eminent because all is sordid and vile about them; as lights are more discerned in a thick darkness than a faint shadow. Now, because they speak all they can (however unfitly), they are thought to have the greater copy; where the learned use ever election and a mean, they look back to what they intended at first, and make all an even and proportioned body. The true artificer will not run away from Nature as he were afraid of her, or depart from life and the likeness of truth, but speak to the capacity of his hearers. And tho his language differ from the vulgar somewhat, it shall not fly from all humanity, with the Tamerlanes and Tamer-chams of the late age, which had nothing in them but the scenical strutting and furious vociferation to warrant them to the ignorant gapers. He knows

it is his only art so to carry it as none but artificers perceive it. In the meantime, perhaps, he
is called barren, dull, lean, a poor writer or by
what contumelious word can come in their cheeks,
by these men who, without labor, judgment,
knowledge, or almost sense, are received or preferred before him. He gratulates them and their
fortune. Another age, or juster men, will acknowledge the virtues of his studies, his wisdom
in dividing, his subtlety in arguing, with what
strength he doth inspire his readers, with what
sweetness he strokes them; in inveighing, what
sharpness; in jest, what urbanity he uses; how
he doth reign in men's affections; how invade
and break in upon them, and makes their minds
like the thing he writes. Then in his elocution
to behold what word is proper, which hath ornaments, which height, what is beautifully translated, where figures are fit, which gentle, which
strong, to show the composition manly; and how
he hath avoided faint, obscure, obscene, sordid,
humble, improper, or effeminate phrase; which is
not only praised of the most, but commended
(which is worse), especially for that it is naught.

IZAAK WALTON

Born in 1593, died in 1683; an ironmonger in London in 1618; his home in Fleet Street in 1624, and from 1628 to 1644 in Chancery Lane, where he had Dr. John Donne, whose life he wrote, for friend and neighbor; living at Clerkenwell in 1653, when he published "The Compleat Angler"; after the Restoration lived at Winchester and Salisbury; wrote lives of Donne, Wotton, Hooker, Herbert and Sanderson.

1

THE ANTIQUITY OF ANGLING [1]

PISCATOR—O sir, doubt not that angling is an art: is it not an art to deceive a trout with an artificial fly? a trout that is more sharp-sighted than any hawk you have named, and more watchful and timorous than your high-mettled merlin is bold; and yet I doubt not to catch a brace or two to-morrow for a friend's breakfast. Doubt not, therefore, sir, but that angling is an art, and an art worth your learning. The question is rather, whether you be capable of learning it? for angling is somewhat like poetry—men are to be born so: I mean, with inclinations to it, tho both may be heightened by discourse and practise; but he that hopes to be a good angler must not only bring an inquiring, searching, observing wit, but he must bring a large measure of hope and patience, and a love and propensity to the

[1] From Part I, Chap. I of "The Compleat Angler."

art itself; but having once got and practised it, then doubt not but angling will prove to be so pleasant that it will prove to be like virtue, a reward to itself.

Venator—Sir, I am now become so full of expectation, that I long much to have you proceed, and in the order you propose.

Piscator—Then first, for the antiquity of angling, of which I shall not say much, but only this: some say it is as ancient as Deucalion's flood,[2] others, that Belus,[3] who was the first inventor of godly and virtuous recreations, was the first inventor of angling; and some others say—for former times have had their disquisitions about the antiquity of it—that Seth, one of the sons of Adam, taught it to his sons, and that by them it was derived to posterity; others say that he left it engraven on those pillars which he erected, and trusted to preserve the knowledge of the mathematics, music, and the rest of that precious knowledge and those useful arts, which by Gods appointment or allowance and his noble industry were thereby preserved from perishing in Noah's flood.

These, sir, have been the opinions of several men that have possibly endeavored to make angling more ancient than is needful, or may well be warranted; but for my part, I shall content myself in telling you that angling is much more

[2] Deucalion was a legendary king of Phythia in Thessaly. According to the legend, a deluge having been sent by Zeus, Deucalion, by advice of his father, built a wooden chest in which he and his wife were saved, landing after nine days on Mt. Parnassus. By them the human race, destroyed in the deluge, was renewed.

[3] A mythological person, son of Poseidon.

ancient than the Incarnation of our Savior: for in the prophet Amos, mention is made of fish-hooks; and in the book of Job, which was long before the days of Amos—for that book is said to be writ by Moses—mention is made also of fish-hooks, which must imply anglers in those times.

But, my worthy friend, as I would rather prove myself a gentleman by being learned and humble, valiant and inoffensive, virtuous and communicable, than by any fond ostentation of riches; or, wanting those virtues myself, boast that these were in my ancestors (and yet I grant that where a noble and ancient descent and such merit meet in any man, it is a double dignification of that person);—so if this antiquity of angling, which for my part I have not forced, shall, like an ancient family, be either an honor or an ornament to this virtuous art which I profess to love and practise, I shall be the gladder that I made an accidental mention of the antiquity of it, of which I shall say no more, but proceed to that just commendation which I think it deserves.

And for that, I shall tell you that in ancient times a debate hath arisen, and it remains yet unresolved: whether the happiness of man in this world doth consist more in contemplation or action?

Concerning which, some have endeavored to maintain their opinion of the first, by saying that the nearer we mortals come to God by way of imitation, the more happy we are. And they say that God enjoys himself only by a contemplation of his own infiniteness, eternity, power, and goodness, and the like. And upon this ground, many cloisteral men of great learning and devotion prefer contemplation before action. And many of the fathers seem to approve this opinion, as may appear in their commentaries upon the words of our Savior to Martha (Luke x : 41, 42).

And on the contrary, there want not men of equal authority and credit, that prefer action to be the more excellent; as namely, experiments in physic, and the application of it, both for the ease and prolongation of man's life; by which each man is enabled to act and do good to others, either to serve his country or do good to particular persons. And they say also that action is doctrinal, and teaches both art and virtue, and is a maintainer of human society; and for these, and other like reasons, to be preferred before contemplation.

Concerning which two opinions, I shall forbear to add a third by declaring my own; and rest myself contented in telling you, my very worthy friend, that both these meet together, and do most properly belong to the most honest, ingenious, quiet, and harmless art of angling.

And first I shall tell you what some have observed, and I have found it to be a real truth—that the very sitting by the river's side is not only the quietest and fittest place for contemplation, but will invite an angler to it; and this seems to be maintained by the learned Peter Du Moulin, who in his discourse on the fulfilling of prophecies, observes that when God intended to reveal any future events or high notions to His prophets, He then carried them either to the deserts or the sea-shore, that having so separated them from amidst the press of people and business, and the cares of the world, He might settle their mind in a quiet repose, and there make them fit for revelation.

II

OF THE TROUT[*]

THE trout is a fish highly valued both in this and foreign nations; he may be justly said, as the old poet said of wine, and we English say of venison, to be a generous fish: a fish that is so like the buck that he also has his seasons; for it is observed, that he comes in and goes out of season with the stag and buck. Gesner says his name is of German offspring, and says he is a fish that feeds clean and purely, in the swiftest streams, and on the hardest gravel; and that he may justly contend with all fresh-water fish, as the mullet may with all sea-fish, for precedency and daintiness of taste, and that being in right season, the most dainty palates have allowed precedency to him.

And before I go further in my discourse, let me tell you, that you are to observe, that as there be some barren does that are good in summer, so there be some barren trouts that are good in winter; but there are not many that are so, for usually they be in their perfection in the month of May, and decline with the buck. Now you are to take notice, that in several coun-

[*] From Chapter IV of "The Compleat Angler."

tries, as in Germany and in other parts, compared to ours, fish differ much in their bigness and shape, and other ways, and so do trouts: It is well known that in Lake Leman, the lake of Geneva, there are trouts taken of three cubits long, as is affirmed by Gesner, a writer of good credit; and Mercator says, the trouts that are taken in the lake of Geneva are a great part of the merchandise of that famous city. And you are further to know, that there be certain waters, that breed trouts remarkable both for their number and smallness. I know a little brook in Kent that breeds them to a number incredible, and you may take them twenty or forty in an hour, but none greater than about the size of a gudgeon: there are also in divers rivers, especially that relate to or be near to the sea, as Winchester, or the Thames about Windsor, a little trout called samlet, or skegger trout (in both which places I have caught twenty or forty at a standing), that will bite as fast and as freely as minnows; these be by some taken to be young salmon; but in those waters they never grow to be bigger than a herring.

There is also in Kent, near to Canterbury, a trout called there a Fordidge trout, a trout that bears the name of the town where it is usually caught, that is accounted the rarest of fish; many of them near the bigness of a salmon, but known by their different color; and in their best season they cut very white; and none of these have been known to be caught with an angle, unless it were one that was caught by Sir George Hastings, an excellent angler, and now with God: and he hath told me, he thought *that* trout bit not for hunger but wantonness; and it is rather to be believed, because both he, then, and many others before him, have been curious to search into their bellies, what the food was by which they lived, and have found out nothing by which they might satisfy their curiosity.

Concerning which you are to take notice, that it is reported by good authors, that grasshoppers, and some fish, have no mouths, but are nourished and take breath by the porousness of their gills, man knows not how: and this may be believed, if we consider that when the raven hath hatched her eggs, she takes no further care, but leaves her young ones to the care of the God of nature, who is said, in the Psalms, "to feed the young ravens that call upon Him." And they be kept alive and fed by dew, or worms that breed in their nests, or some other ways that we mortals know not; and this may be believed of the Fordidge trout, which, as it is said of the stork (Jerem. viii : 7), that "he knows his season," so he knows his times, I think almost his day of coming into the river out of the sea, where he lives, and, it is like, feeds nine months of the year, and fasts three in the river of Fordidge. And you are to note that those townsmen are very punctual in observing the time of beginning to fish for them, and boast much that their river affords a trout that exceeds all others. And just so does Sussex boast of several fish; as namely, a Shelsey cockle, a Chichester lobster, an Arundel mullet, and an Amerly trout.

And now for some confirmation of the Fordidge trout: you are to know that this trout is thought to eat nothing in the fresh water; and it may be better believed, because it is well known, that swallows and bats and wagtails, which are called half-year birds, and not seen to fly in England for six months in the year, but about Michaelmas leave us for a better climate than this; yet some of them that have been left behind their fellows, have been found many thousands at a time, in hollow trees, or clay caves; where they have been observed to live and sleep out the whole winter without meat; and so Albertus observes, that there is one kind of frog that hath her mouth naturally shut up about the end of August, and that she lives so all the winter; and tho it be strange to some, yet it is known to too many among us to be doubted.

And so much for these Fordidge trouts, which never afford an angler sport, but either live their time of being in the fresh water by their meat formerly got in the sea (not unlike the swallow or frog), or by the virtue of the fresh water only; or, as the birds of Paradise and the chameleon are said to live, by the sun and the air.

There is also in Northumberland a trout called a bull trout, of a much greater length and bigness than any in the southern parts. And there are, in many rivers that relate to the sea, salmon trouts, as much different from others, both in shape and in their spots, as we see sheep in some countries differ one from another in their shape and bigness, and in the fineness of their wool. And certainly, as some pastures breed larger sheep, so do some rivers, by reason of the ground over which they run, breed larger trouts.

Now the next thing that I will commend to

your consideration is, that the trout is of a more sudden growth than other fish. Concerning which, you are also to take notice, that he lives not so long as the perch and divers other fishes do, as Sir Francis Bacon hath observed in his "History of Life and Death."[5]

And now you are to take notice, that he is not like the crocodile, which if he lives never so long, yet always thrives till his death. And you are to know, that he will about, especially before, the time of his spawning, get almost miraculously through weirs and flood-gates against the streams; even through such high and swift places as is almost incredible. Next, that the trout usually spawns about October or November, but in some rivers a little sooner or later; which is the more observable, because most other fish spawn in the spring or summer, when the sun hath warmed both the earth and the water, and made it fit for generation. And you are to note, that he continues many months out of season; for it may be observed of the trout, that he is like the buck or the ox, that he will not be fat in many months, tho he go in the very same pasture that horses do, which will be fat in one month; and so you may observe, that most other fishes recover strength, and grow sooner far and in season, than the trout doth.

And next you are to note, that till the sun gets to such a height as to warm the earth and the water, the trout is sick and lean, and lousy, and unwholesome; for you shall in winter find him to have a big head, and then to be lank, and thin, and lean; at which time many of them

[5] The "Historia Vitæ et Mortis," published in 1623.

have sticking on them sugs, or trout-lice, which is a kind of worm, in shape like a clove or pin, with a big head, and sticks close to him and sucks his moisture; those I think the trout breeds himself, and never thrives till he frees himself from them, which is when warm weather comes; and then, as he grows stronger, he gets from the dead, still water, into the sharp streams, and the gravel, and there tubs off these worms or lice; and then as he grows stronger, so he gets him into swifter and swifter streams, and there lies at the watch for any fly or minnow that comes near to him; and he especially loves the May-fly, which is bred of the cod-worm or caddis; and these make the trout bold and lusty, and he is usually fatter and better meat at the end of that month (May) than at any time of the year.

III

THE DEATH OF GEORGE HERBERT [6]

AT the time of Mr. Duncon's leaving Mr. Herbert—which was about three weeks before his death—his old and dear friend Mr. Woodnot came from London to Bemerton, and never left him till he had seen him draw his last breath, and closed his eyes on his death-bed. In this time of his decay, he was often visited and prayed for by all the clergy that lived near to him, especially by his friends the Bishop and Prebends

[6] Author of "The Temple; Sacred Poems and Private Ejaculations," published in 1633, the year of Herbert's death.

of the Cathedral Church in Salisbury; but by none more devoutly than his wife, his three nieces — then a part of his family — and Mr. Woodnot, who were the sad witnesses of his daily decay; to whom he would often speak to this purpose:

"I now look back upon the pleasures of my life past, and see the content I have taken in beauty, in wit, in music, and pleasant conversation, are now all past by me like a dream, or as a shadow that returns not, and are now all become dead to me, or I to them; and I see, that as my father and generation hath done before me, so I also shall now suddenly (with Job) make my bed also in the dark; and I praise God I am prepared for it; and I praise Him that I am not to learn patience now I stand in such need of it; and that I have practised mortification, and endeavored to die daily, that I might not die eternally; and my hope is, that I shall shortly leave this valley of tears, and be free from all fevers and pain; and, which will be a more happy condition, I shall be free from sin, and all the temptations and anxieties that attend it: and this being past, I shall dwell in the New Jerusalem; dwell there with men made perfect; dwell where these eyes shall see my Master and Savior Jesus; and with Him see my dear mother, and all my relations and friends. But I must die, or not come to that happy place. And this is my content, that I am going daily towards it: and that every day which I have lived, hath taken a part of my appointed time from me; and that I shall live the less time, for having lived this and the day past."

These, and the like expressions, which he uttered often, may be said to be his enjoyment of Heaven before he enjoyed it. The Sunday before his death, he rose suddenly from his bed or couch, called for one of his instruments, took it into his hand and said,

> My God, my God,
> My music shall find Thee,
>   And every string
> Shall have His attribute to sing.

and having tuned it, he played and sung:

> The Sundays of man's life,
> Threaded together on time's string,
> Make bracelets to adorn the wife
> Of the eternal glorious King:
> On Sundays Heaven's door stands ope;
> Blessings are plentiful and rife,
>   More plentiful than hope.

Thus he sung on earth such hymns and anthems, as the angels, and he, and Mr. Farrer, now sing in heaven. Thus he continued meditating, and praying, and rejoicing, till the day of his death; and on that day said to Mr. Woodnot, "My dear friend, I am sorry I have nothing to present to my merciful God but sin and misery; but the first is pardoned, and a few hours will now put a period to the latter; for I shall suddenly go hence, and be no more seen." Upon which expression Mr. Woodnot took occasion to remember him of the reedifying Layton Church, and his many acts of mercy. To which he made answer, saying, "They be good works, if they be sprinkled with the blood of Christ, and not otherwise.''

After this discourse he became more restless, and his soul seemed to be weary of her earthly tabernacle; and this uneasiness became so visible, that his wife, his three nieces, and Mr. Woodnot, stood constantly about his bed, beholding him with sorrow, and an unwillingness to lose the sight of him, whom they could not hope to see much longer. As they stood thus beholding him, his wife observed him breathe faintly, and with much trouble, and observed him to fall into a sudden agony; which so surprized her, that she fell into a sudden passion, and required of him to know how he did. To which his answer was, ''that he had passed a conflict with his last enemy, and had overcome him by the merits of his Master Jesus.'' After which answer, he looked up, and saw his wife and nieces weeping to an extremity, and charged them, if they loved him to withdraw into the next room, and there pray every one alone for him; for nothing but their lamentations could make his death uncomfortable. To which request their sighs and tears would not suffer them to make any reply; but they yielded him a sad obedience, leaving only with him Mr. Woodnot and Mr. Bostock.

Immediately after they had left him, he said to Mr. Bostock, ''Pray, Sir, open that door, then look into that cabinet, in which you may easily find my last will, and give it into my hand''; which being done, Mr. Herbert delivered it into the hand of Mr. Woodnot, and said, ''My old friend, I here deliver you my last will, in which you will find that I have made you my sole executor for the good of my wife and nieces; and I desire you to show kindness to them, as they shall need it; I do not desire you to be just; for I know you will be so for your own sake; but I charge you, by the religion of our friendship, to be careful of them.'' And having obtained Mr. Woodnot's promise to be so, he said, ''I am now ready to die.'' After which words, he said, ''Lord, forsake me not now my strength faileth me: but grant me mercy for the merits of my Jesus. And now, Lord—Lord, now receive my soul.'' And with those words he breathed forth his divine soul, without any apparent disturbance, Mr. Woodnot and Mr. Bostock attending his last breath, and closing his eyes.

JAMES HOWELL

Born in 1595, died in 1666; best known as author of the "Letters" (1645-1655); edited a French and English dictionary; and compiled a polyglot dictionary.

I

THE BUCENTAUR CEREMONY IN VENICE[1]

THESE wishes come to you from Venice, a place where there is nothing wanting that heart can wish; renowned Venice, the admired'st city in the world, a city that all Europe is bound unto, for she is her greatest rampart against that huge eastern tyrant, the Turk, by sea; else, I believe, he had overrun all Christendom by this time. Against him this city hath performed notable exploits, and not only against him, but divers others: she hath restored emperors to their thrones, and popes to their chairs, and with her galleys often preserved St. Peter's bark from sinking: for which, by way of reward, one of his successors espoused her to the sea, which marriage is solemnly renewed every year in solemn procession by the Doge and all the Clarissimos, and a gold ring cast into the sea out of the great

[1] From the "Familiar Letters," the date of this letter being "Venice, 25th June, 1621."

galeasse, called the Bucentoro,[2] wherein the first
ceremony was performed by the pope himself,
above three hundred years since, and they say
it is the self-same vessel still, tho often put upon
the careen and trimmed. This made me think of
that famous ship at Athens; nay, I fell upon an
abstracted notion in philosophy, and a specula-
tion touching the body of men, which being in
perpetual flux, and a kind of succession of decays,
and consequently requiring, ever and anon, a
restoration of what it loseth of the virtue of the
former aliment, and what was converted after
the third concoction into a blood and fleshy substance, which, as in all other sublunary bodies
that have internal principles of heat, useth to
transpire, breathe out, and waste away through
invisible pores, by exercise, motion, and sleep,
to make room still for a supply of new nurriture:
I fell, I say, to consider whether our bodies may
be said to be of like condition with this Bucentoro, which, tho it be reputed still the same vessel, yet I believe there's not a foot of that timber
remaining which it had upon the first dock, having been, as they tell me, so often planked and
ribbed, caulked and pieced.

In like manner, our bodies may be said to be
daily repaired by new sustenance, which begets
new blood, and consequently new spirits, new
humors, and, I may say, new flesh; the old, by
continual deperdition and insensible perspira-

---

[2] Now written Bucentaur, the state ship of the Venetian
republic. The ceremony of "espousing the sea" dates from
the twelfth century. The last of the Bucentaur ships of
Venice was destroyed by Napoleon in 1798. It was the
third that had been built for Venice.

tions, evaporating still out of us, and giving way
to fresh; so that I make a question whether, by
reason of these perpetual reparations and ac-
cretions, the body of man may be said to be the
same numerical body in his old age that he had
in his manhood, or the same in his manhood that
he had in his youth, the same in his youth that
he carried about with him in his childhood, or
the same in his childhood which he wore first in
the womb. I make a doubt whether I had the
same identical, individually numerical body, when
I carried a calf-leather satchel to school in Here-
ford, as when I wore a lambskin hood in Oxford;
or whether I have the same mass of blood in
my veins, and the same flesh, now in Venice,
which I carried about me three years since, up
and down London streets, having, in lieu of beer
and ale, drunk wine all this while, and fed upon
different viands. Now, the stomach is like a
crucible, for it hath a chemical kind of virtue to
transmute one body into another, to transsub-
stantiate fish and fruits into flesh within and
about us; but tho it be questionable whether I
wear the same flesh which is fluxible, I am sure
my hair is not the same, for you may remember
I went flaxen-haired out of England, but you
shall find me returned with a very dark brown,
which I impute not only to the heat and air of
those hot countries I have eat my bread in, but
to the quality and difference of food: you will
say that hair is but an excrementitious thing,
and makes not to this purpose; moreover, methinks I hear thee say that this may be true
only in the blood and spirits, or such fluid parts,
not in the solid and heterogeneal parts.

But I will press no further at this time this philosophical notion, which the sight of Bucentoro infused into me, for it hath already made me exceed the bounds of a letter, and, I fear me, to trespass too much upon your patience; I leave the further disquisition of this point to your own contemplations, who are a far riper philosopher than I, and have waded deeper into and drunk more of Aristotle's well. But to conclude, tho it be doubtful whether I carry about me the same body or no in all points that I had in England, I am well assured I bear still the same mind, and therein I verify the old verse:

"Cœlum non animum mutant qui trans mare currunt."

"The air, but not the mind, they change,
Who in outlandish countries range."

For, what alterations soever happen in this microcosm, in this little world, this small bulk and body of mine, you may be confident that nothing shall alter my affections, specially towards you, but that I will persevere still the same—the very same.

II

THE CITY OF ROME IN 1621 [*]

I AM now come to Rome, and Rome, they say, is every man's country; she is called *Communis Patria*, for every one that is within the compass of the Latin Church finds himself here, as it

[*] From the "Familiar Letters."

or writ from the pope in these words: "*Creamus te socium regibus, superiorem ducibus, et fratrem nostrum.*"[6] If a cardinal bishop should be questioned for any offense, there must be twenty-four witnesses produced against him. The Bishop of Ostia hath most privilege of any other, for he consecrates and installs the pope, and goes always next to him. All these cardinals have the repute of princes, and besides other incomes, they have the annats of benefices to support their greatness.

For point of power, the pope is able to put 50,000 men in the field, in case of necessity, besides his naval strength in galleys. We read how Paul III sent Charles III twelve thousand foot and five hundred horse. Pius V sent a greater aid to Charles IX; and for riches, besides the temporal dominions he hath in all the countries before named, the datany or dispatching of bulls, the triennial subsidies, annats, and other ecclesiastical rights, mount to an unknown sum; and it is a common saying here, that as long as the pope can finger a pen, he can want no pence. Pius V, notwithstanding his expenses in buildings, left four millions in the Castle of Saint Angelo in less than five years; more, I believe, than this Gregory XV will, for he hath many nephews; and better is it to be the pope's nephew, than to be a favorite to any prince in Christendom.

Touching the temporal government of Rome, and oppidan affairs, there is a pretor and some choice citizens, which sit in the Capitol. Among

---

[6] These words mean "We create thee companion to kings, superior to dukes, and our brother.

other pieces of policy, there is a synagog of
Jews permitted here—as in other places of Italy
—under the pope's nose, but they go with a
mark of distinction in their hats; they are tol-
erated for advantage of commerce, wherein the
Jews are wonderful dexterous—tho most of them
be only brokers and Lombardeers; and they are
held to be here as the cynic held women to be—
malum necessarium. . . .

Present Rome may be said to be but a monument of Rome past, when she was in that flourish
that St. Austin desired to see her in. She who
tamed the world, tamed herself at last, and
falling under her own weight, fell to be a prey
to time; yet there is a providence seems to have
a care of her still; for tho her air be not so
good, nor her circumjacent soil so kindly as it
was, yet she hath wherewith to keep life and
soul together still, by her ecclesiastical courts,
which is the sole cause of her peopling now; so
that it may be said, when the pope came to be
her head, she was reduced to her first principles;
for as a shepherd was founder, so a shepherd is
still governor and preserver.

SIR THOMAS BROWNE

Born in 1605, died in 1682; educated at Oxford, Padua and
Leyden; in 1633 made Doctor of Medicine; settled at
Norwich in 1637; knighted in 1671; his "Religio Medici"
published in 1643; author of several other works.

I

OF CHARITY IN JUDGMENTS[1]

Now for that other virtue of charity, without
which faith is a mere notion and of no existence,
I have ever endeavored to nourish the merciful
disposition and humane inclination I borrowed
from my parents, and regulate it to the written
and prescribed laws of charity: and if I hold the
true anatomy of myself, I am delineated and
naturally framed to such a piece of virtue; for
I am of a constitution so general that it consorts
and sympathizeth with all things: I have no
antipathy, or rather idiosyncrasy, in diet, humor,
air, anything. I wonder not at the French for
their dishes of frogs, snails, and toadstools; nor
at the Jews for locusts and grasshoppers; but
being amongst them, make them my common
viands, and I find they agree with my stomach
as well as theirs. I could digest a salad gathered
in a churchyard as well as in a garden. I cannot
start at the presence of a serpent, scorpion,
lizard, or salamander: at the sight of a toad or

[1] From the "Religio Medici."

viper I find in me no desire to take up a stone
to destroy them. I feel not in myself those
common antipathies that I can discover in others;
those national repugnances do not touch me, nor
do I behold with prejudice the French, Italian,
Spaniard, or Dutch; but where I find their actions in balance with my countrymen's, I honor,
love, and embrace them in the same degree.

I was born in the eighth climate, but seem for
to be framed and constellated unto all: I am no
plant that will not prosper out of a garden; all
places, all airs, make unto me one country; I
am in England, everywhere, and under any meridian; I have been shipwrecked, yet am not enemy with the sea or winds; I can study, play
or sleep in a tempest. In brief, I am averse
from nothing: my conscience would give me
the lie if I should absolutely detest or hate any
essence but the devil; or so at least abhor anything but that we might come to composition.
If there be any among those common objects
of hatred I do contemn and laugh at, it is that
great enemy of reason, virtue, and religion—
the multitude: that numerous piece of mon-
strosity which, taken asunder, seem men and the
reasonable creatures of God, but confused together, make but one great beast and a mon-
strosity more prodigious than Hydra: it is no
breach of charity to call these fools; it is the
style all holy writers have afforded them, set
down by Solomon in canonical Scripture, and a
point of our faith to believe so. Neither in the
name of multitude do I only include the base
and minor sort of people: there is a rabble even
amongst the gentry, a sort of plebeian heads,

be confident of no end—which is the peculiar of that necessary essence that can not destroy itself—and the highest strain of omnipotency, to be so powerfully constituted as not to suffer even from power of itself; all others have a dependent being and within the reach of destruction. But the sufficiency of Christian immortality frustrates all earthly glory, and the quality of either states after death, makes a folly of posthumous memory. God, who can only destroy our souls, and hath assured our resurrection, either of our bodies or names, hath directly promised no duration. Wherein there is so much of chance, that the boldest expectants have found unhappy frustration; and to hold long subsistences, seems but a scape in oblivion. But man is a noble animal, splendid in ashes, and pompous in the grave, solemnizing nativities and deaths with equal luster, nor omitting ceremonies of bravery in the infamy of nature.

Life is a pure flame, and we live by an invisible sum within us. A small fire sufficeth for life, great flames seemed too little after death, while men vainly affected precious pyres, and to burn like Sardanapalus; but wisdom of funeral laws found the folly of prodigal blazes, and reduced undoing fires unto the rule of sober obsequies, wherein few could be so mean as not to provide wood, pitch, a mourner, and an urn.

Five languages secured not the epitaph of Gordianus.[4] The man of God lives longer without a tomb than any by one, invisibly interred by angels, and adjudged to obscurity, tho not

[4] A Roman emperor whose epitaph was cut in Greek, Latin, Hebrew, Egyptian and Arabic.

without some marks directing human discovery. Enoch and Elias, without either tomb or burial, in an anomalous state of being, are the great examples of perpetuity, in their long and living memory, in strict account being still on this side death, and having a late part yet to act upon this stage of earth. If in the decretory term of the world we shall not all die but be changed, according to received translation, the last day will make but few graves; at least quick resurrections will anticipate lasting sepultures. Some graves will be opened before they be quite closed, and Lazarus be no wonder. When many that feared to die, shall groan that they can die but once, the dismal state is the second and living death, when life puts despair on the damned; when men shall wish the coverings of mountains, not of monuments, and annihilations shall be courted.

While some have studied monuments, others have studiously declined them, and some have been so vainly boisterous, that they durst not acknowledge their graves; wherein Alaric seems most subtle, who had a river turned to hide his bones at the bottom. Even Sylla, that thought himself safe in his urn, could not prevent revenging tongues, and stones thrown at his monument. Happy are they whom privacy makes innocent, who deal so with men in this world, that they are not afraid to meet them in the next; who, when they die, make no commotion among the dead, and are not touched with that poetical taunt of Isaiah.

Pyramids, arches, obelisks, were but the irregularities of vainglory, and wild enormities of ancient magnanimity. But the most magnanimous resolution rests in the Christian religion, which trampleth upon pride, and sits on the neck of ambition, humbly pursuing that infallible perpetuity, unto which all others must diminish their diameters, and be poorly seen in angles of contingency.

Pious spirits who passed their days in raptures of futurity, made little more of this world, than the world that was before it, while they lay obscure in the chaos of pre-ordination, and night of their fore-beings. And if any have been so happy as truly to understand Christian annihilation, ecstasies, exolution, liquefaction, transformation, the kiss of the spouse, gustation of God, and ingression into the divine shadow, they have already had an handsome anticipation of heaven; the glory of the world is surely over, and the earth is ashes unto them.

To subsist in lasting monuments, to live in their productions, to exist in their names and predicament of chimeras, was large satisfaction unto old expectations, and made one part of their elysiums. But all this is nothing in the metaphysics of true belief. To live indeed, is to be again ourselves, which being not only a hope, but an evidence in noble believers, 'tis all one to lie in St. Innocent's church-yard, as in the sands of Egypt. Ready to be anything, in the ecstasy of being ever, and as content with six foot as the moles of Hadrianus.[5]

[5] Now the Castle of St. Angelo in Rome.

JOHN MILTON

Born in 1608, died in 1674; visited Italy in 1638; began his political writings in 1640; Latin Secretary to the Commonwealth in 1649; became totally blind in 1652; spared at the Restoration under the Indemnity Act; published "Paradise Lost" in 1667.

I

ON HIS OWN LITERARY AMBITION [a]

AFTER I had, from my first years, by the ceaseless diligence and care of my father (whom God recompense!), been exercised to the tongues, and some sciences, as my age would suffer, by sundry masters and teachers, both at home and at the schools, it was found that whether aught was imposed me by them that had the overlooking, or betaken to of my own choice in English, or other tongue, prosing or versing, but chiefly the latter, the style, by certain vital signs it had, was likely to live. But much latelier, in the private academies of Italy, whither I was favored to resort, perceiving that some trifles which I had in memory, composed at under twenty or thereabout—for the manner is, that every one must give some proof of his wit and reading there—met with acceptance above what was looked for; and other things which I had shifted, in scarcity of books and conveniences, to patch up among them, were received with written encomiums,

[a] From "The Reason of Church Government."

which the Italian is not forward to bestow on men of this side the Alps, I began thus far to assent both to them and divers of my friends here at home; and not less to an inward prompting, which now grew daily upon me, that by labor and intent study, which I take to be my portion in this life, joined to the strong propensity of nature, I might perhaps leave something so written, to after-times, as they should not willingly let it die.

These thoughts at once possest me, and these other, that if I were certain to write as men buy leases, for three lives and downward, there ought no regard be sooner had than to God's glory, by the honor and instruction of my country. For which cause, and not only for that I knew it would be hard to arrive at the second rank among the Latins, I applied myself to that resolution which Ariosto followed against the persuasions of Bembo,[2] to fix all the industry and art I could unite to the adorning of my native tongue; not to make verbal curiosities the end—that were a toilsome vanity; but to be an interpreter, and relater of the best and sagest things among mine own citizens throughout this island, in the mother dialect. That what the greatest and choicest wits of Athens, Rome, or modern Italy, and those Hebrews of old did for their country, I, in my proportion, with this over and above, of being a Christian, might do for

[2] Bembo, cardinal and man of letters, was born in Venice in 1470 and died in 1547. He wrote poems and other works, and was the friend of the first men of culture in his age. Several popes honored him, and he had the intimate friendship of Lucretia Borgia.

mine; not caring to be once named abroad, tho
perhaps I could attain to that, but content with
these British islands as my world; whose fortune hath hitherto been, that if the Athenians,
as some say, made their small deeds great and
renowned by their eloquent writers, England
hath had her noble achievements made small by
the unskilful handling of monks and mechanics.

Time serves not now, and perhaps I might seem
too profuse, to give any certain account of what
the mind at home, in the spacious circuits of
her musing, hath liberty to propose to herself,
tho of highest hope and hardest attempting.
Whether that epic form, whereof the two poems
of Homer, and those other two of Virgil and
Tasso are a diffuse, and the book of Job a brief,
model; or whether the rules of Aristotle herein
are strictly to be kept, or nature to be followed,
which in them that know art, and use judgment,
is no transgression, but an enriching of art.
And, lastly, what king or knight before the Con-
quest might be chosen, in whom to lay the pattern of a Christian hero. And as Tasso gave
to a prince of Italy his choice, whether he would
command him to write of Godfrey's[3] expedition
against the infidels, or Belisarius against the
Goths, or Charlemagne against the Lombards;
if to the instinct of nature and the emboldening
of art aught may be trusted, and that there be
nothing adverse in our climate, or the fate of
this age, it haply would be no rashness, from an
equal diligence and inclination, to present the

[3] Godfrey of Bouillon, leader of the First Crusade, died in
Jerusalem in 1100, a year after he had defeated the Sultan
of Egypt at Ascalon.

like offer in our own ancient stories. Or whether those dramatic constitutions, wherein Sophocles and Euripides reign, shall be found more doctrinal and exemplary to a nation.

The Scripture also affords us a fine pastoral drama in the Song of Solomon, consisting of two persons, and a double chorus, as Origen[*] rightly judges; and the Apocalypse of St. John is the majestic image of a high and stately tragedy, shutting up and intermingling her solemn scenes and acts with a seven-fold chorus of hallelujahs and harping symphonies. And this my opinion, the grave authority of Paræus, commenting that book, is sufficient to confirm. Or if occasion shall lead, to imitate those magnific odes and hymns, wherein Pindarus and Callimachus are in most things worthy, some others in their frame judicious, in their matter most, and end faulty. But those frequent songs throughout the law and prophets, beyond all these, not in their divine argument alone, but in the very critical art of composition, may be easily made appear, over all the kinds of lyric poesy, to be incomparable.

These abilities, wheresoever they be found, are the inspired gift of God, rarely bestowed, but yet to some—tho most abuse—in every nation: and are of power, besides of the office of a pulpit, to inbreed and cherish in a great people the seeds of virtue and public civility; to allay the perturbations of the mind, and set the affections in right tune; to celebrate in glorious and lofty hymns the throne and equipage of God's

---

[*] Chief among the Greek fathers of the church, born about 185 A.D. and the author of many books.

almightiness, and what he suffers to be wrought with high providence in his church; to sing victorious agonies of martyrs and saints, the deeds and triumphs of just and pious nations, doing valiantly through faith against the enemies of Christ; to deplore the general relapses of kingdoms and states from justice and God's true worship.

Lastly, whatsoever in religion is holy and sublime, in virtue amiable or grave, whatsoever hath passion or admiration in all the changes of that which is called fortune from without, or the wily subtleties and refluxes of man's thoughts from within; all these things, with a solid and treatable smoothness, to paint out and describe; teaching over the whole book of sanctity and virtue, through all the instances of example, with such delight to those, especially of soft and delicious temper, who will not so much as look upon Truth herself, unless they see her elegantly drest, that whereas the paths of honesty and good life appear now rugged and difficult, tho they be indeed easy and pleasant, they would then appear to all men both easy and pleasant, tho they were rugged and difficult indeed.

II

A COMPLETE EDUCATION DEFINED [5]

AND seeing every nation affords not experience and tradition enough for all kind of learning, therefore we are chiefly taught the languages of those people who have at any time been most industrious after wisdom; so that language is but the instrument conveying to us things useful to be known. And tho a linguist should pride himself to have all the tongues that Babel cleft the world into, yet, if he have not studied the solid things in them, as well as the words and lexicons, he were nothing so much to be esteemed a learned man, as any yeoman or tradesman competently wise in his mother dialect only. Hence appear the many mistakes which have made learning generally so unpleasing and so unsuccessful: first, we do amiss to spend seven or eight years merely in scraping together so much miserable Latin and Greek, as might be learned otherwise easily and delightfully in one year.

And that which casts our proficiency therein so much behind, is our time lost partly in too oft idle vacancies given both to schools and universities; partly in a preposterous exaction, forcing the empty wits of children to compose themes, verses, and orations, which are the acts of ripest judgment, and the final work of a head filled by long reading and observing, with elegant maxims and copious invention. These are not

[5] From the "Tractate on Education."

matters to be wrung from poor striplings, like blood out of the nose, or the plucking of untimely fruit; besides the ill habit which they get of wretched barbarizing against the Latin and Greek idiom, with their untutored Anglicisms, odious to be read, yet not to be avoided without a well-continued and judicious conversing among pure authors digested, which they scarce taste: whereas, if after some preparatory grounds of speech by their certain forms got into memory, they were led to the praxis thereof in some chosen short book lessoned thoroughly to them, they might then forthwith proceed to learn the substance of good things and arts in due order, which would bring the whole language quickly into their power. This I take to be the most rational and most profitable way of learning languages, and whereby we may best hope to give account to God of our youth spent herein.

And for the usual method of teaching arts, I deem it to be an old error of universities, not yet well recovered from the scholastic grossness of barbarous ages, that instead of beginning with arts most easy—and those be such as are most obvious to the sense—they present their young unmatriculated novices at first coming with the most intellective abstractions of logic and metaphysics, so that they having but newly left those grammatic flats and shallows where they stuck unreasonably to learn a few words with lamentable construction, and now on the sudden transported under another climate, to be tossed and turmoiled with their unballasted wits in fathomless and unquiet deeps of controversy, do for the most part grow into hatred and contempt of learning, mocked and deluded all this while with ragged notions and babblements, while they expected worthy and delightful knowledge; till poverty or youthful years call them importunately their several ways, and hasten them, with the sway of friends, either to an ambitious and mercenary, or ignorantly zealous divinity; some allured to the trade of law, grounding their purposes, not on the prudent and heavenly contemplation of justice and equity, which was never taught them, but on the promising and pleasing thoughts of litigious terms, fat contentions, and flowing fees; others betake them to state affairs, with souls so unprincipled in virtue and true generous breeding, that flattery and courtshifts, and tyrannous aphorisms, appear to them the highest points of wisdom; instilling their barren hearts with a conscientious slavery; if, as I rather think, it be not feigned. Others, lastly, of a more delicious and airy spirit, retire themselves, knowing no better, to the enjoyments of ease and luxury, living out their days in feasts and jollity; which, indeed, is the wisest and the safest course of all these, unless they were with more integrity undertaken. And these are the errors, and these are the fruits of misspending our prime youth at schools and universities as we do, either in learning mere words, or such things chiefly as were better unlearned.

I shall detain you now no longer in the demonstration of what we should do, but straight conduct you to a hillside, while I will point you out the right path of a virtuous and noble education; laborious, indeed, at the first ascent, but else so smooth, so green, so full of goodly prospect and melodious sounds on every side, that the harp of Orpheus was not more charming. I doubt not but ye shall have more ado to drive our dullest and laziest youth, our stocks and stubs, from the infinite desire of such a happy nurture, than we have now to hale and drag our choicest and hopefulest wits to that asinine feast of sow thistles and brambles which is commonly set before them, as all the food and entertainment of their tenderest and most docile age.

I call, therefore, a complete and generous education, that which fits a man to perform justly, skilfully, and magnanimously, all the offices, both private and public, of peace and war.

III

ON READING IN HIS YOUTH[6]

He who would not be frustrate of his hope to write well hereafter in laudable things ought himself to be a true poem; that is, a composition and pattern of the best and honorablest things; not presuming to sing high praises of heroic men, or famous cities, unless he have in himself the experience and the practise of all that which is praiseworthy. These reasonings, together with a certain niceness of nature, an honest haughtiness, and self-esteem either of what I was, or what I might be (which let envy

[6] From the "Apology for Smectymnus."

call pride), and lastly that modesty, whereof, tho not in the title-page, yet here I may be excused to make some beseeming profession; all these uniting the supply of their natural aid together kept me still above those low descents of mind, beneath which he must deject and plunge himself, that can agree to salable and unlawful prostitutions.

Next (for hear me out now, readers), that I may tell ye whither my younger feet wandered; I betook me among those lofty fables and romances, which recount in solemn cantos the deeds of knighthood founded by our victorious kings, and from hence had in renown over all Christendom. There I read it in the oath of every knight, that he should defend to the expense of his best blood, or of his life, if it so befell him, the honor and chastity of virgin or matron; from whence even then I learned what a noble virtue chastity sure must be, to the defense of which so many worthies, by such a dear adventure of themselves, had sworn. And if I found in the story afterward, any of them, by word or deed, breaking that oath, I judged it the same fault of the poet, as that which is attributed to Homer, to have written indecent things of the gods. Only this my mind gave me, that every free and gentle spirit, without that oath, ought to be born a knight, nor needed to expect the gilt spur, or the laying of a sword upon his shoulder to stir him up both by his counsel and his arms, to secure and protect the weakness of any attempted chastity. So that even these books, which to many others have been the fuel of wantonness and loose living, I can not think how, unless

by divine indulgence, proved to me so many in-
citements, as you have heard to the love and
stedfast observation of that virtue which abhors
the society of bordelloes.

IV

IN DEFENSE OF BOOKS[7]

I DENY not, but that it is of greatest concern-
ment in the Church and Commonwealth, to have
a vigilant eye how books demean themselves as
well as men; and thereafter to confine, imprison,
and do sharpest justice on them as malefactors.
For books are not absolutely dead things, but
do contain a potency of life in them to be as
active as that soul was whose progeny they are;
nay, they do preserve as in a vial the purest
efficacy and extraction of that living intellect
that bred them. I know they are as lively, and
as vigorously productive, as those fabulous drag-
on's teeth; and being sown up and down, may
chance to spring up armed men. And yet, on
the other hand, unless wariness be used, as good
almost kill a man as kill a good book. Who
kills a man kills a reasonable creature, God's
image; but he who destroys a good book, kills
reason itself, kills the image of God, as it were
in the eye. Many a man lives a burden to the
earth; but a good book is the precious life-blood
of a master-spirit, embalmed and treasured up
on purpose to a life beyond life. 'Tis true, no age

---

[7] From the "Areopagitica."

can restore a life, whereof perhaps there is no great loss; and revolutions of ages do not oft recover the loss of a rejected truth, for the want of which whole nations fare the worse.

We should be wary therefore what persecution we raise against the living labors of public men, how we spill that seasoned life of man, preserved and stored up in books; since we see a kind of homicide may be thus committed, sometimes a martyrdom, and if it extend to the whole impression, a kind of massacre; whereof the execution ends not in the slaying of an elemental life, but strikes at that ethereal and fifth essence, the breath of reason itself, slays an immortality rather than a life. But lest I should be condemned of introducing license, while I oppose licensing, I refuse not the pains to be so much historical, as will serve to show what hath been done by ancient and famous commonwealths against this disorder, till the very time that this project of licensing crept out of the inquisition, was catched up by our prelates and hath caught some of our presbyters.

In Athens, where books and wits were ever busier than in any other part of Greece, I find but only two sorts of writings which the magistrate cared to take notice of; those either blasphemous and atheistical, or libelous. Thus the books of Protagoras were by the judges of Areopagus commanded to be burnt, and himself banished the territory for a discourse begun with his confessing not to know "whether there were gods, or whether not." And against defaming, it was agreed that none should be traduced by name, as was the manner of Vetus Comœdia, whereby we may guess how they censured libeling. And this course was quick enough, as Cicero writes, to quell both the desperate wits of other atheists, and the open way of defaming, as the event showed. Of other sects and opinions, tho tending to voluptuousness, and the denying of Divine Providence, they took no heed.

Therefore we do not read that either Epicurus, or that libertine school of Cyrene, or what the Cynic impudence uttered, was ever questioned by the laws. Neither is it recorded that the writings of those old comedians were supprest tho the acting of them were forbid; and that Plato commended the reading of Aristophanes, the loosest of them all, to his royal scholar Dionysius, is commonly known, and may be excused, if holy Chrysostom, as is reported, nightly studied so much the same author and had the art to cleanse a scurrilous vehemence into the style of a rousing sermon.

That other leading city of Greece, Lacedemon, considering that Lycurgus, their lawgiver, was so addicted to elegant learning, as to have been the first that brought out of Ionia the scattered works of Homer, and sent the poet Thales from Crete to prepare and mollify the Spartan surliness with his smooth songs and odes, the better to plant among them law and civility, it is to be wondered how useless and unbookish they were, minding nought but the feats of war. There needed no licensing of books among them, for they disliked all but their own laconic apothegms, and took a slight occasion to chase Archilochus out of their city, perhaps for composing in a higher strain than their own soldierly ballads and roundels could reach to. Or if it were for his broad verses, they were not therein so cautious, but were as dissolute in their promiscuous conversing; whence Euripides affirms in "Andromache," that their women were all unchaste. Thus much may give us light after what sort of books were prohibited among the Greeks.

The Romans also for many ages trained up only to a military roughness, resembling most the Lacedæmonian guise, knew of learning little but what their twelve tables, and the Pontific College with their augurs and flamens taught them in religion and law, so unacquainted with other learning, that when Carneades and Critolaus, with the Stoic Diogenes, coming ambassadors to Rome, took thereby occasion to give the city a taste of their philosophy, they were suspected for seducers by no less a man than Cato the Censor, who moved it in the Senate to dismiss them speedily, and to banish all such Attic babblers out of Italy. But Scipio and others of the noblest senators withstood him and his old Sabine austerity; honored and admired the men; and the censor himself at last, in his old age, fell to the study of that whereof before he was so scrupulous. And yet at the same time, Nævius and Plautus, the first Latin comedians, had filled the city with all the borrowed scenes of Menander and Philemon. Then began to be considered there also what was to be done to libelous books and authors; for Nævius was quickly cast into prison for his unbridled pen, and released by the tribunes upon his recantation; we read also that libels were burnt, and the makers punished by Augustus. The like severity, no doubt, was used, if aught were impiously written against their esteemed gods. Except in these two points, how the world went in books, the magistrate kept no reckoning.

V

A NOBLE AND PUISSANT NATION[8]

LORDS and Commons of England, consider what nation it is whereof ye are, and whereof ye are the governors: a nation not slow and dull, but of a quick, ingenious and piercing spirit, acute to invent, subtle and sinewy to discourse, not beneath the reach of any point, the highest that human capacity can soar to. Therefore the studies of Learning in her deepest sciences have been so ancient and so eminent among us, that writers of good antiquity and ablest judgment have been persuaded that even the school of Pythagoras and the Persian wisdom took beginning from the old philosophy of this island. And that wise and civil Roman, Julius Agricola, who governed once here for Cæsar, preferred the natural wits of Britain before the labored studies of the French. Nor is it for nothing that the grave and frugal Transylvanian sends out yearly from as far as the mountainous borders of Russia, and beyond the Hercynian wilderness, not their youth, but their staid men, to learn our language and our theologic arts.

[8] From the "Areopagitica."

135

Yet that which is above all this, the favor and the love of Heaven we have great argument to think in a peculiar manner propitious and propending toward us. Why else was this nation chosen before any other, that out of her, as out of Sion, should be proclaimed and sounded forth the first tidings and trumpet of Reformation to all Europe? And had it not been the obstinate perverseness of our prelates against the divine and admirable spirit of Wycliff, to suppress him as a schismatic and innovator, perhaps neither the Bohemian Huss and Jerome, no nor the name of Luther or of Calvin, had been ever known: the glory of reforming all our neighbors had been completely ours. But now, as our obdurate clergy have with violence demeaned the matter, we are become hitherto the latest and backwardest scholars, of whom God offered to have made us the teachers. Now once again by all concurrence of signs, and by the general instinct of holy and devout men, as they daily and solemnly express their thoughts, God is decreeing to begin some new and great period in His Church, even to the reforming of Reformation itself: what does He then but reveal Himself to His servants, and as His manner is, first to His Englishmen? I say, as His manner is, first to us, tho we mark not the method of His counsels, and are unworthy.

Behold now this vast city: a city of refuge, the mansion house of liberty, encompassed and surrounded with His protection; the shop of war hath not there more anvils and hammers waking, to fashion out the plates and instruments of armed Justice in defense of beleaguered Truth,

than there be pens and heads there, sitting by
their studious lamps, musing, searching, revolv-
ing new notions and ideas wherewith to present,
as with their homage and their fealty, the ap-
proaching Reformation: others as fast reading,
trying all things, assenting to the force of reason
and convincement. What could a man require
more from a nation so pliant and so prone to
seek after knowledge? What wants there to
such a towardly and pregnant soil, but wise and
faithful laborers, to make a knowing people, a
nation of prophets, of sages, and of worthies?
We reckon more than five months yet to harvest;
there need not be five weeks; had we but eyes
to lift up, the fields are white already.

Where there is much desire to learn, there of
necessity will be much arguing, much writing,
many opinions; for opinion in good men is but
knowledge in the making. Under these fantastic
terrors of sect and schism, we wrong the earnest
and zealous thirst after knowledge and understanding which God hath stirred up in this city.
What some lament of, we rather should rejoice
at, should rather praise this pious forwardness
among men, to reassume the ill-reputed care of
their religion into their own hands again. A
little generous prudence, a little forbearance of
one another, and some grain of charity might
win all these diligences to join, and unite in
one general and brotherly search after Truth;
could we but forego this prelatical tradition of
crowding free consciences and Christian liberties
into canons and precepts of men. I doubt not,
if some great and worthy stranger should come
among us, wise to discern the mold and temper

of a people, and how to govern it, observing the high hopes and aims, the diligent alacrity of our extended thoughts and reasonings in the pursuance of truth and freedom, but that he would cry out as Pyrrhus did, admiring the Roman docility and courage: If such were my Epirots, I would not despair the greatest design that could be attempted, to make a church or kingdom happy.

Yet these are the men cried out against for schismatics and sectaries; as if, while the temple of the Lord was building, some cutting, some squaring the marble, others hewing the cedars, there should be a sort of irrational men who could not consider there must be many schisms and many dissections made in the quarry and in the timber, ere the house of God can be built. And when every stone is laid artfully together, it can not be united into a continuity, it can but be contiguous in this world; neither can every piece of the building be of one form; nay rather the perfection consists in this, that, out of many moderate varieties and brotherly dissimilitudes that are not vastly disproportional, arises the goodly and the graceful symmetry that commends the whole pile and structure.

Let us therefore be more considerate builders, more wise in spiritual architecture, when great reformation is expected. For now the time seems come, wherein Moses the great prophet may sit in heaven rejoicing to see that memorable and glorious wish of his fulfilled, when not only our seventy elders, but all the Lord's people, are become prophets. No marvel then tho some men, and some good men too perhaps, but young in goodness, as Joshua then was, envy them. They fret, and out of their own weakness are in agony, lest these divisions and subdivisions will undo us. The adversary again applauds, and waits the hour: When they have branched themselves out, saith he, small enough into parties and partitions, then will be our time. Fool! he sees not the firm root out of which we all grow, tho into branches: nor will beware until he see our small divided maniples cutting through at every angle of his ill-united and unwieldy brigade. And that we are to hope better of all these supposed sects and schisms, and that we shall not need that solicitude, honest perhaps tho over-timorous of them that vex in this behalf, but shall laugh in the end at those malicious applauders of our differences, I have these reasons to persuade me. . . .

Methinks I see in my mind a noble and puissant nation rousing herself like a strong man after sleep, and shaking her invincible locks. Methinks I see her as an eagle mewing her mighty youth, and kindling her undazzled eyes at the full midday beam: purging and unscaling her long-abused sight at the fountain itself of heavenly radiance; while the whole noise of timorous and flocking birds, with those also that love the twilight, flutter about, amazed at what she means, and in their envious gabble would prognosticate a year of sects and schisms.

What should ye do then? should ye suppress all this flowery crop of knowledge and new light sprung up and yet springing daily in this city? should ye set an oligarchy of twenty engrossers over it, to bring a famine upon our minds again, when we shall know nothing but what is measured to us by their bushel? Believe it, Lords and Commons, they who counsel ye to such a suppressing do as good as bid ye suppress yourselves; and I will soon show how. If it be desired to know the immediate cause of all this free writing and free speaking, there can not be assigned a truer than your own mild and free and humane government. It is the liberty, Lords and Commons, which your own valorous and happy counsels have purchased us, liberty which is the nurse of all great wits; this is that which hath rarefied and enlightened our spirits like the influence of heaven; this is that which hath enfranchised, enlarged and lifted up our apprehensions degrees above themselves.

Ye can not make us now less capable, less knowing, less eagerly pursuing of the truth, unless ye first make yourselves, that made us so, less the lovers, less the founders of our true liberty. We can grow ignorant again, brutish, formal and slavish, as ye found us; but you then must first become that which ye can not be, oppressive, arbitrary and tyrannous, as they were from whom ye have freed us. That our hearts are now more capacious, our thoughts more erected to the search and expectation of greatest and exactest things, is the issue of your own virtue propagated in us; ye can not suppress that, unless ye reinforce an abrogated and merciless law, that fathers may dispatch at will their own children. And who shall then stick closest to ye, and excite others? not he who takes up arms for coat and conduct, and his four nobles of Danegelt. Altho I dispraise not the defense

of just immunities, yet love my peace better, if
that were all. Give me the liberty to know, to
utter, and to argue freely according to conscience,
above all liberties.

VI

OF FUGITIVE AND CLOISTERED VIRTUE[*]

I CAN NOT praise a fugitive and cloistered virtue, unexercised and unbreathed, that never
sallies out and sees her adversary, but slinks
out of the race, where that immortal garland is
to be run for, not without dust and heat. As-
suredly we bring not innocence into the world,
we bring impurity much rather; that which puri-
fies us is trial, and trial is by what is contrary.
That virtue therefore which is but a youngling
in the contemplation of evil, and knows not the
utmost that vice promises to her followers, and
rejects it, is but a blank virtue, not a pure; her
whiteness is but an excremental whiteness.
Which was the reason why our sage and serious
poet Spenser, whom I dare be known to think a
better teacher than Scotus or Aquinas, describing
true temperance under the person of Guion,
brings him in with his palmer through the cave
of Mammon, and the bower of earthly bliss, that
he might see and know, and yet abstain. Since
therefore the knowledge and survey of vice is
in this world so necessary to the constituting of
human virtue, and the scanning of error to the

[*] From the "Areopagitica."

confirmation of truth, how can we more safely, and with less danger, scout into the regions of sin and falsity than by reading all manner of tractates and hearing all manner of reason? And this is the benefit which may be had of books promiscuously read.

But of the harm that may result hence three kinds are usually reckoned. First, is feared the infection that may spread; but then all human learning and controversy in religious points must remove out of the world, yea the Bible itself; for that ofttimes relates blasphemy not nicely, it describes the carnal sense of wicked men not unelegantly, it brings in holiest men passionately murmuring against Providence through all the arguments of Epicurus: in other great disputes it answers dubiously and darkly to the common reader. And ask a Talmudist what ails the modesty of his marginal Keri, that Moses and all the prophets can not persuade him to pronounce the textual Chetiv. For these causes we all know the Bible itself put by the Papist into the first rank of prohibited books. The ancientest fathers must be next removed, as Clement of Alexandria, and that Eusebian book of Evangelic preparation, transmitting our ears through a hoard of heathenish obscenities to receive the Gospel. Who finds not that Irenæus, Epiphanius, Jerome, and others discover more heresies than they well confute, and that oft for heresy which is the truer opinion?

Nor boots it to say for these, and all the heathen writers of greatest infection, if it must be thought so, with whom is bound up the life of human learning, that they writ in an unknown tongue, so long as we are sure those languages are known as well to the worst of men, who are both most able, and most diligent to instil the poison they suck, first into the courts of princes, acquainting them with the choicest delights, and criticisms of sin. As perhaps did that Petronius whom Nero called his Arbiter, the master of his revels; and the notorious ribald of Arezzo,[10] dreaded and yet dear to the Italian courtiers. I name not him for posterity's sake, whom Henry VIII named in merriment his vicar of hell. By which compendious way all the contagion that foreign books can infuse will find a passage to the people far easier and shorter than an Indian voyage, tho it could be sailed either by the north of Cataio eastward, or of Canada westward, while our Spanish licensing gags the English press never so severely.

But on the other side that infection which is from books of controversy in religion is more doubtful and dangerous to the learned than to the ignorant; and yet those books must be permitted untouched by the licenser. It will be hard to instance where any ignorant man hath been ever seduced by papistical book in English, unless it were commended and expounded to him by some of that clergy: and indeed all such tractates, whether false or true, are as the prophecy of Isaiah was to the eunuch, not to be understood without a guide.

[10] A reference to Pietro Aretino, born in 1492, died in 1557, a notoriously indecent writer and adventurer. Henry VIII once sent him 300 crowns.

LORD CLARENDON

Born in 1608, died in 1674; entered Parliament in 1640;
chancellor of the Exchequer in 1643; chief adviser of
Charles the First during the Civil War; lord chancellor 1660-
67; impeached and banished; his "History of the Rebellion"
published in 1702-04.

OF CHARLES I[1]

But it will not be unnecessary to add a short
character of his person, that posterity may know
the inestimable loss which the nation then under-
went, in being deprived of a prince whose example would have had a greater influence upon
the manners and piety of the nation, than the
most strict laws can have. To speak first of
his private qualifications as a man, before the
mention of his princely and royal virtues; he
was, if ever any, the most worthy of the title
of an honest man; so great a lover of justice,
that no temptation could dispose him to a wrong-
ful action, except it was so disguised to him
that he believed it to be just. He had a tenderness and compassion of nature which restrained
him from ever doing a hard-hearted thing; and,
therefore, he was so apt to grant pardon to malefactors, that the judges of the land represented
to him the damage and insecurity to the public
that flowed from such his indulgence. And then
he restrained himself from pardoning either
murders or highway robberies, and quickly dis-

[1] From the "History of the Rebellion."

cerned the fruits of his severity by a wonderful reformation of those enormities. He was very punctual and regular in his devotions; he was never known to enter upon his recreations or sports, tho never so early in the morning, before he had been at public prayers; so that on hunting-days his chaplains were bound to a very early attendance. He was likewise very strict in observing the hours of his private cabinet devotions, and was so severe an exacter of gravity and reverence in all mention of religion, that he could never endure any light or profane word, with what sharpness of wit soever it was covered; and tho he was well pleased and delighted with reading verses made upon any occasion, no man durst bring before him anything that was profane or unclean. That kind of wit had never any countenance then. He was so great an example of conjugal affection, that they who did not imitate him in that particular, durst not brag of their liberty; and he did not only permit, but direct his bishops to prosecute those scandalous vices, in the ecclesiastical courts, against persons of eminence, and near relation to his service.

His kingly virtues had some mixture and allay that hindered them from shining in full luster, and from producing those fruits they should have been attended with. He was not in his nature very bountiful, tho he gave very much. This appeared more after the Duke of Buckingham's death,[2] after which those showers fell

---

[2] George Villiers, first Duke of Buckingham, the chief minister of Charles, was assassinated by John Felton in 1628.

very rarely; and he paused too long in giving,
which made those to whom he gave less sensible
of the benefit. He kept state to the full, which
made his court very orderly, no man presuming
to be seen in a place where he had no pretence
to be. He saw and observed men long before he
received them about his person; and did not love
strangers, nor very confident men. He was a
patient hearer of causes, which he frequently
accustomed himself to at the council board, and
judged very well, and was dexterous in the medi-
ating part; so that he often put an end to causes
by persuasion, which the stubbornness of men's
humors made dilatory in courts of justice.

He was very fearless in his person; but, in
his riper years, not very enterprising. He had
an excellent understanding, but was not confident
enough of it; which made him oftentimes change
his own opinion for a worse, and follow the
advice of men that did not judge so well as himself. This made him more irresolute than the
conjuncture of his affairs would admit; if he
had been of a rougher and more imperious nature, he would have found more respect and duty.
And his not applying some severe cures to ap-
proaching evils proceeded from the lenity of his
nature, and the tenderness of his conscience,
which, in all cases of blood, made him choose the
softer way, and not hearken to severe counsels,
how reasonable soever urged. This only restrained him from pursuing his advantage.

As he excelled in all other virtues, so in temperance he was so strict that he abhorred all
debauchery to that degree, that, at a great festival solemnity, where he once was, when very

many of the nobility of the English and Scots were entertained, being told by one who withdrew from thence, what vast drafts of wine they drank, and "that there was one earl who had drunk most of the rest down, and was not himself moved or altered," the king said "that he deserved to be hanged"; and that earl coming shortly after into the room where his majesty was, in some gaiety, to shew how unhurt he was from that battle, the king sent some one to bid him withdraw from his majesty's presence; nor did he in some days after appear before him.

So many miraculous circumstances contributed to his ruin, that men might well think that heaven and earth conspired it. Tho he was, from the first declension of his power, so much betrayed by his own servants, that there were very few who remained faithful to him, yet that treachery proceeded not always from any treasonable purpose to do him any harm, but from particular and personal animosities against other men. And afterward, the terror all men were under of the parliament, and the guilt they were conscious of themselves, made them watch all opportunities to make themselves gracious to those who could do them good; and so they became spies upon their master, and from one piece of knavery were hardened and confirmed to undertake another, till at last they had no hope of preservation but by the destruction of their master.

And after all this, when a man might reasonably believe that less than a universal defection of three nations could not have reduced a great king to so ugly a fate, it is most certain

boys as schoolmasters, to be tied to the school, as Cooper's Dictionary [2] and Scapula's Lexicon are chained to the desk therein; and tho great scholars, and skilful in other arts, are bunglers in this. But God, of his goodness, hath fitted several men for several callings, that the necessity of church and state, in all conditions, may be provided for. So that he who beholds the fabric thereof, may say, God hewed out the stone, and appointed it to lie in this very place, for it would fit none other so well, and here it doth most excellent. And thus God moldeth some for a schoolmaster's life, undertaking it with desire and delight, and discharging it with dexterity and happy success.

He studieth his scholars' natures as carefully as they their books; and ranks their dispositions into several forms. And tho it may seem difficult for him in a great school to descend to all particulars, yet experienced schoolmasters may quickly make a grammar of boys' natures, and reduce them all—saving some few exceptions—to these general rules:

1. Those that are ingenious and industrious. The conjunction of two such planets in a youth presage much good unto him. To such a lad a frown may be a whipping, and a whipping a death; yea, where their master whips them once, shame whips them all the week after. Such natures he useth with all gentleness.

2. Those that are ingenious and idle. These

---

[2] Cooper's "Latin Dictionary" was first published in 1565 and was long a standard school-book in England. It received the special patronage of Queen Elizabeth. Cooper was made Bishop of Winchester in 1584.

think with the hare in the fable, that running
with snails—so they count the rest of their
schoolfellows—they shall come soon enough to
the post, tho sleeping a good while before their
starting. O! a good rod would finely take them
napping!

3. Those that are dull and diligent. Wines,
the stronger they be, the more lees they have
when they are new. Many boys are muddy-
headed till they be clarified with age, and such
afterward prove the best. Bristol diamonds are
both bright, and squared, and pointed by nature,
and yet are soft and worthless; whereas Orient
ones in India are rough and rugged naturally.
Hard, rugged, and dull natures of youth acquit
themselves afterward the jewels of the country,
and therefore their dulness at first is to be borne
with, if they be diligent. That schoolmaster deserves to be beaten himself who beats nature
in a boy for a fault. And I question whether
all the whipping in the world can make their
parts which are naturally sluggish rise one min-
ute before the hour nature hath appointed.

4. Those that are invincibly dull, and negligent
also. Correction may reform the latter, not
amend the former. All the whetting in the world
can never set a razor's edge on that which hath
no steel in it. Such boys he consigneth over to
other professions. Shipwrights and boat-makers
will choose those crooked pieces of timber which
other carpenters refuse. Those may make excellent merchants and mechanics who will not
serve for scholars.

He is able, diligent, and methodical in his
teaching; not leading them rather in a circle

than forward. He minces his precepts for children to swallow, hanging clogs on the nimbleness of his own soul, that his scholars may go along with him.

He is and will be known to be an absolute monarch in his school. If cockering mothers proffer him money to purchase their sons an exemption from his rod—to live, as it were, in a peculiar, out of their master's jurisdiction—with disdain he refuseth it, and scorns the late custom in some places of commuting whipping into money, and ransoming boys from the rod at a set price. If he hath a stubborn youth, correction-proof, he debaseth not his authority by contesting with him, but fairly, if he can, puts him away before his obstinacy hath infected others.

He is moderate in inflicting deserved correction. Many a schoolmaster better answereth the name *paidotribes* than *paidagogos*, rather tearing his scholars' flesh with whipping than giving them good education. No wonder if his scholars hate the Muses, being presented unto them in the shapes of fiends and furies.

JEREMY TAYLOR

Baptized in 1613, died in 1667; son of a barber; educated
at Cambridge; chaplain to Charles I during the Civil War;
after the Restoration made Bishop of Down and Connor, and
a member of the Irish Privy Council; his "Holy Living"
published in 1650, and "Holy Dying" in 1651.

THE BENEFITS OF ADVERSITY [1]

No man is more miserable than he that hath
no adversity—that man is not tried whether he
be good or bad: and God never crowns those
virtues which are only faculties and dispositions;
but every act of virtue is an ingredient into
reward. And we see many children fairly
planted, whose parts of nature were never drest
by art, nor called from the furrows of their
first possibilities by discipline and institution,
and they dwell forever in ignorance, and con-
verse with beasts; and yet if they had been drest
and exercised, might have stood at the chairs
of princes, or spoken parables amongst the rulers
of cities. Our virtues are but in the seed when
the grace of God comes upon us first; but this
grace must be thrown into broken furrows, and
must twice feel the cold and twice feel the heat,
and be softened with storms and showers, and
then it will arise into fruitfulness and harvests.
And what is there in the world to distinguish
virtues from dishonors, or the valor of Cæsar

[1] From the "Rules and Exercises of Holy Dying."

153

from the softness of the Egyptian eunuchs, or that can make anything rewardable but the labor and the danger, the pain and the difficulty? Virtue could not be anything but sensuality if it were the entertainment of our senses and fond desires; and Apicius had been the noblest of all the Romans, if feeding and great appetite and despising the severities of temperance had been the work and proper employment of a wise man. But otherwise do fathers and otherwise do mothers handle their children. These soften them with kisses and imperfect noises, with the pap and breast-milk of soft endearments; they rescue them from tutors and snatch them from discipline; they desire to keep them fat and warm, and their feet dry, and their bellies full: and then the children govern, and cry, and prove fools and troublesome, so long as the feminine republic does endure.

But fathers—because they design to have their children wise and valiant, apt for counsel or for arms—send them to severe governments, and tie them to study, to hard labor, and afflictive contingencies. They rejoice when the bold boy strikes a lion with his hunting-spear, and shrinks not when the beast comes to affright his early courage. Softness is for slaves and beasts, for minstrels and useless persons, for such who can not ascend higher than the state of a fair ox or a servant entertained for vainer offices; but the man that designs his son for nobler employments —to honors and to triumphs, to consular dignities and presidencies of councils—loves to see him pale with study or panting with labor, hardened with suffrance or eminent by dangers. And so God dresses us for heaven: he loves to see us struggling with a disease, and resisting the devil, and contesting against the weaknesses of nature, and against hope to believe in hope— resigning ourselves to God's will, praying Him to choose for us, and dying in all things but faith and its blest consequents; *ut ad officium cum periculo sinus prompti*—and the danger and the resistance shall endear the office. For so have I known the boisterous north wind pass through the yielding air, which opened its bosom, and appeased its violence by entertaining it with easy compliance in all the region of its reception; but when the same breath of heaven hath been checked with the stiffness of a tower, or the united strength of a wood, it grew mighty and dwelt there, and made the highest branches stoop and make a smooth path for it on the top of all its glories.

ABRAHAM COWLEY

Born in 1618, died in 1667; son of a stationer; educated
at Cambridge and Oxford; identified himself with the
Royalists; fled with the Queen to France in 1646; returned
to England in 1656, settled afterward at Chertsey; highly
esteemed in his own day as a poet; his works first collected
in 1668.

I

OF OBSCURITY [1]

WHAT a brave privilege is it to be free from
all contentions, from all envying or being envied,
from receiving and from paying all kind of
ceremonies! It is, in my mind, a very delightful
pastime for two good and agreeable friends to
travel up and down together, in places where
they are by nobody known, nor know anybody.
It was the case of Æneas and his Achates, when
they walked invisibly about the fields and streets
of Carthage. Venus herself

A veil of thickened air around them cast,
That none might know, or see them, as they
    passed.   VIRG. 1 Æn.

The common story of Demosthenes's confession,
that he had taken great pleasure in hearing of
a tanker-woman say, as he passed: "This is that
Demosthenes," is wonderfully ridiculous from
so solid an orator. I myself have often met

[1] From the "Essays."

with that temptation to vanity, if it were any; but am so far from finding it any pleasure, that it only makes me run faster from the place, till I get, as it were, out of sight-shot. Democritus[2] relates, and in such a manner as if he gloried in the good fortune and commodity of it, that, when he came to Athens, nobody there did so much as take notice of him; and Epicurus lived there very well, that is, lay hid many years in his gardens, so famous since that time, with his friend Metrodorus: after whose death, making, in one of his letters, a kind commemoration of the happiness which they two had enjoyed together, he adds at last that he thought it no disparagement to those great felicities of their life, that, in the midst of the most talked-of and talking country in the world, they had lived so long, not only without fame, but almost without being heard of; and yet, within a very few years afterward, there were no two names of men more known or more generally celebrated.

If we engage into a large acquaintance and various familiarities, we set open our gates to the invaders of most of our time; we expose our life to a quotidian ague of frigid impertinences, which would make a wise man tremble to think of. Now, as for being known much by sight, and pointed at, I can not comprehend the honor that lies in that; whatsoever it be, every mountebank has it more than the best doctor, and the hangman more than the lord chief-justice of a city. Every creature has it, both of nature and art, if it be anyways extraor-

[2] Democritus was born about 460 B.C. and died about 357. He was often known as "The Laughing Philosopher."

dinary. It was as often said: "This is that Bucephalus,"[3] or, "This is that Incitatus,"[4] when they were led prancing through the streets, as, "This is that Alexander," or, "This is that Domitian"; and truly, for the latter, I take Incitatus to have been a much more honorable beast than his master, and more deserving the consulship than he the empire.

I love and commend a true good fame, because it is the shadow of virtue: not that it doth any good to the body which it accompanies, but it is an efficacious shadow, and like that of St. Peter, cures the diseases of others. The best kind of glory, no doubt, is that which is reflected from honesty, such as was the glory of Cato and Aristides; but it was harmful to them both, and is seldom beneficial to any man whilst he lives; what it is to him after his death, I can not say, because I love not philosophy merely notional and conjectural, and no man who has made the experiment has been so kind as to come back to inform us. Upon the whole matter, I account a person who has a moderate mind and fortune, and lives in the conversation of two or three agreeable friends, with little commerce in the world besides, who is esteemed well enough by his few neighbors that know him, and is truly irreproachable by anybody; and so, after a healthful quiet life, before the great inconveniences of old age, goes more silently out of it than he came in—for I would not have him so much as cry in the exit: this innocent

---

[3] The famous horse ridden by Alexander the Great.

[4] A horse ridden by the Roman Emperor Domitian.

deceiver of the world, as Horace calls him, this
muta persona, I take to have been more happy
in his part than the greatest actors that fill the
stage with show and noise; nay, even than Augustus himself, who asked, with his last breath,
whether he had not played his farce very well.

II

OF PROCRASTINATION[6]

I AM glad that you approve and applaud my
design of withdrawing myself from all tumult
and business of the world, and consecrating the
little rest of my time to those studies to which
nature had so motherly inclined me, and from
which fortune, like a step-mother, has so long
detained me. But, nevertheless, you say (which
but is *ærugo mera*, a rust which spoils the good
metal it grows upon)—but you say you would
advise me not to precipitate that resolution, but
to stay a while longer with patience and complaisance, till I had gotten such an estate as
might accord me—according to the saying of that
person, whom you and I love very much, and
would believe as soon as another man—*cum dig-
nitate otium*. This were excellent advice to
Joshua, who could bid the sun stay too. But
there's no fooling with life, when it is once
turned beyond forty: the seeking for a fortune
then is but a desperate after-game; 'tis a hun-

[6] From the "Essays."

dred to one if a man fling two sixes, and recover all; especially if his hand be no luckier than mine.

There is some help for all the defects of fortune; for if a man can not attain to the length of his wishes, he may have his remedy by cutting of them shorter. Epicurus writes a letter to Idomeneus—who was then a very powerful, wealthy, and, it seems, a bountiful person—to recommend to him, who had made so many rich, one Pythocles, a friend of his, whom he desired might be made a rich man too; "but I entreat you that you would not do it just the same way as you have done to many less deserving persons; but in the most gentlemanly manner of obliging him, which is, not to add anything to his estate, but to take something from his desires."

The sum of this is, that for the certain hopes of some conveniences, we ought not to defer the execution of a work that is necessary; especially when the use of those things which we would stay for may otherwise be supplied, but the loss of time never recovered; nay, farther yet, tho we were sure to obtain all that we had a mind to, tho we were sure of getting never so much by continuing the game, yet when the light of life is so near going out, and ought to be so precious, *le jeu ne vaut pas la chandelle*, the play is not worth the expense of the candle; after having been long tossed in a tempest, if our masts be standing, and we have still sail and tackling enough to carry us to our port, it is no matter for the want of streamers and topgallants.

GEORGE FOX

Born in 1624, died in 1691; founder of the Society of
Friends; son of a weaver, apprenticed to a shoemaker; became an itinerant lay preacher at the age of 25, completing
the organization of the Society of Friends in 1669; made
missionary journeys to Scotland, Ireland, and West Indies,
Holland and North America (1671-72); frequently impris-
oned for infraction of the laws against Conventicles.

AN INTERVIEW WITH OLIVER CROM-
WELL [1]

AFTER Captain Drury had lodged me at the
Mermaid, over against the Mews at Charing
Cross, he went to give the Protector an account
of me. When he came to me again, he told me
the Protector required that I should promise not
to take up a carnal sword or weapon against
him or the government, as it then was; and
that I should write it in what words I saw good,
and set my hand to it. I said little in reply
to Captain Drury, but the next morning I was
moved of the Lord to write a paper to the Protector, by the name of Oliver Cromwell, wherein
I did, in the presence of the Lord God, declare
that I did deny the wearing or drawing of a
"carnal sword, or any other outward weapon,
against him or any man; and that I was sent
of God to stand a witness against all violence,
and against the works of darkness, and to turn
people from darkness to light; to bring them

[1] From the "Journal."

from the occasion of war and fighting to the peaceable Gospel, and from being evil-doers, which the magistrates' sword should be a terror to." When I had written what the Lord had given me to write, I set my name to it, and gave it to Captain Drury to hand to Oliver Cromwell, which he did. After some time, Captain Drury brought me before the Protector himself at Whitehall. It was in a morning, before he was drest; and one Harvey, who had come a little among friends, but was disobedient, waited upon him.

When I came in, I was moved to say: "Peace be in this house"; and I exhorted him to keep in the fear of God, that he might receive wisdom from Him; that by it he might be ordered, and with it might order all things under his hand unto God's glory. I spoke much to him of truth; and a great deal of discourse I had with him about religion, wherein he carried himself very moderately. But he said we quarreled with the priests, whom he called ministers. I told him, "I did not quarrel with them, they quarreled with me and my friends. But, said I, if we own the prophets, Christ, and the apostles, we can not hold up such teachers, prophets, and shepherds, as the prophets, Christ, and the apostles declared against; but we must declare against them by the same power and spirit." Then I shewed him that the prophets, Christ, and the apostles, declared freely, and declared against them that did not declare freely; such as preached for filthy lucre, divined for money, and preached for hire, and were covetous and greedy, like the dumb dogs that could never have enough;

and that they who have the same spirit that Christ, and the prophets, and the apostles had, could not but declare against all such now, as they did then. As I spoke, he several times said it was very good, and it was truth. I told him: "That all Christendom, so called, had the Scriptures, but they wanted the power and spirit that those had who gave forth the Scriptures, and that was the reason they were not in fellowship with the Son, nor with the Father, nor with the Scriptures, nor one with another.

Many more words I had with him, but people coming in, I drew a little back. As I was turning, he catched me by the hand, and with tears in his eyes said: "Come again to my house, for if thou and I were but an hour of a day together, we should be nearer one to the other"; adding, that he wished me no more ill than he did to his own soul. I told him, if he did, he wronged his own soul, and admonished him to harken to God's voice, that he might stand in His counsel, and obey it; and if he did so, that would keep him from hardness of heart; but if he did not hear God's voice, his heart would be hardened. He said it was true. Then I went out; and when Captain Drury came out after me, he told me the lord Protector said I was at liberty, and might go whither I would. Then I was brought into a great hall, where the Protector's gentlemen were to dine. I asked them what they brought me thither for. They said it was by the Protector's order, that I might dine with them. I bid them let the Protector know I would not eat of his bread, nor drink of his drink. When he heard this, he said:

"Now I see there is a people risen that I can not win, either with gifts, honors, offices, or places; but all other sects and people I can." It was told him again, "That we had forsook our own, and were not like to look for such things from him."[2]

[2] Just before Cromwell's death, Fox had another interview with him of which he wrote: "The same day, taking boat, I went down (*up*) to Kingston, and from thence to Hampton Court, to speak with the Protector about the sufferings of friends. I met him riding into Hampton Court Park; and before I came to him, as he rode at the head of his life-guard, I saw and felt a waft (*whiff*) of death go forth against him; and when I came to him he looked like a dead man. After I had laid the sufferings of friends before him, and had warned him according as I was moved to speak to him, he bade me come to his house. So I returned to Kingston, and the next day went up to Hampton Court to speak further with him. But when I came, Harvey, who was one that waited on him, told me the doctors were not willing that I should speak with him. So I passed away, and never saw him more."

Carlyle in his "Life and Letters of Cromwell," quoting this passage, says: "His life, if thou knew it, has not been a merry thing for this man, now or heretofore! I fancy he has been looking this long while to give it up, whenever the Commander-in-chief required. To quit his laborious sentry-post; honorably lay up his arms, and be gone to his rest—all eternity to rest in, George! Was thy own life merry, for example, in the hollow of the tree; clad permanently in leather? And does kingly purple, and governing refractory worlds instead of stitching coarse shoes, make it merrier? The waft of death is not against him, I think—perhaps, against thee, and me, and others, O George, when the Nell Gwynne defender and two centuries of all-victorious cant have come in upon us!"

JOHN BUNYAN

Baptized in 1628, died in 1688; son of a tinker, adopting his father's trade; served two years in the Civil Wars; joined a Non-Conformist body at Bedford about 1645, becoming a traveling preacher in the midland counties; arrested in 1660 under statutes against Non-Conformists and spent several years in jail, where he wrote part of his "Pilgrim's Progress," published in 1678-1684; on being released from prison was licensed to preach and remained pastor at Bedford until he died.

I

A DREAM OF THE CELESTIAL CITY

Now I saw in my dream that by this time the pilgrims were got over the Enchanted Ground, and entering into the country of Beulah, whose air was very sweet and pleasant, the way lying directly through it, they solaced them there for the season. Yea, here they heard continually the singing of birds, and saw every day the flowers appear in the earth, and heard the voice of the turtle in the land. In this country the sun shineth night and day; wherefore it was beyond the Valley of the Shadow of Death, and also out of the reach of Giant Despair; neither could they from this place so much as see Doubting Castle. Here they were within sight of the city they were going to; also here met them some of the inhabitants thereof: for in

---

[1] From "The Pilgrim's Progress."

this land the shining ones commonly walked, because it was upon the borders of Heaven. In this land, also, the contract between the bride and bridegroom was renewed; yea, here, "as the bridegroom rejoiceth over the bride, so did their God rejoice over them." Here they had no want of corn and wine; for in this place they met abundance of what they had sought for in all their pilgrimage. Here they heard voices from out of the city, loud voices, saying: "Say ye to the daughter of Zion, behold thy salvation cometh! Behold, his reward is with him!" Here all the inhabitants of the country called them "the holy people, the redeemed of the Lord, sought out," etc.

Now, as they walked in this land, they had more rejoicing than in parts more remote from the kingdom to which they were bound; and drawing nearer to the city yet, they had a more perfect view thereof: it was built of pearls and precious stones, also the streets thereof were paved with gold; so that, by reason of the natural glory of the city, and the reflection of the sunbeams upon it, Christian with desire fell sick; Hopeful also had a fit or two of the same disease: wherefore here they lay by it a while, crying out, because of their pangs: "If you see my Beloved, tell him that I am sick of love."

But being a little strengthened, and better able to bear their sickness, they walked on their way, and came yet nearer and nearer, where were orchards, vineyards, and gardens, and their gates opened into the highway. Now, as they came up to these places, behold the gardener stood in the way, to whom the pilgrims said:

Whose goodly vineyards and gardens are these?
He answered: They are the King's, and are
planted here for his own delight, and also for
the solace of pilgrims: so the gardener had them
into the vineyards and bid them refresh themselves with dainties; he also shewed them there
the King's walks and arbors, where he delighted
to be; and here they tarried and slept.

Now, I beheld in my dream that they talked
more in their sleep at this time than ever they
did in all their journey; and being in a muse
thereabout, the gardener said even to me: Wherefore musest thou at the matter? It is the nature
of the fruit of the grapes of these vineyards
to go down so sweetly, as to cause the lips of
them that are asleep to speak.

So I saw that when they awoke, they addrest
themselves to go up to the city. But, as I said,
the reflection of the sun upon the city—for the
city was pure gold—was so extremely glorious,
that they could not as yet with open face behold
it, but through an instrument made for that
purpose. So I saw that, as they went on, there
met them two men in raiment that shone like
gold; also their faces shone as the light.

These men asked the pilgrims whence they
came; and they told them. They also asked them
where they had lodged, what difficulties and
dangers, what comforts and pleasures, they had
met with in their way; and they told them. Then
said the men that met them: You have but two
difficulties more to meet with, and then you are
in the city.

Christian and his companion then asked the
men to go along with them; so they told them

that they would. But, said they, you must obtain it by your own faith. So I saw in my dream that they went on together till they came in sight of the gate. . . .

Then I saw in my dream that Christian was in a muse a while. To whom, also, Hopeful added these words: Be of good cheer; Jesus Christ maketh thee whole: and with that Christian brake out with a loud voice—Oh! I see him again; and he tells me: "When thou passest through the waters, I will be with thee; and through the rivers, they shall not overflow thee." Then they both took courage, and the enemy was after that as still as a stone, until they were gone over. Christian, therefore, presently found ground to stand upon, and so it followed that the rest of the river was but shallow; but thus they got over. Now, upon the bank of the river on the other side, they saw the two shining men again, who there waited for them; wherefore, being come out of the river, they saluted them, saying "We are ministering spirits, sent for to minister to those that shall be heirs of salvation." Thus they went along toward the gate. Now you must note that the city stood upon a mighty hill; but the pilgrims went up that hill with ease, because they had these two men to lead them up by the arms; they had likewise left their mortal garments behind them in the river; for tho they went in with them, they came out without them. They therefore went up here with much agility and speed, tho the foundation upon which the city was framed was higher than the clouds.

II

THE DEATH OF VALIANT-FOR-TRUTH AND OF STAND-FAST [2]

It was noised abroad that Mr *Valiant-for-truth* was taken with a Summons by the same Post as the other, and had this for a Token that the Summons was true, That his Pitcher was broken at the Fountain. When he understood it, he called for his Friends, and told them of it. Then said he, I am going to my Fathers, and tho with great difficulty I am got hither, yet now I do not repent me of all the Trouble I have been at to arrive where I am. My Sword I give to him that shall succeed me in my Pilgrimage, and my Courage and Skill to him that can get it. My Marks and Scars I carry with me, to be a witness for me that I have fought his Battles who now will be my Rewarder. When the day that he must go hence was come, many accompanied him to the River-side, into which as he went he said, Death, where is thy Sting? And as he went down deeper he said, Grave, where is thy Victory? So he passed over, and all the Trumpets sounded for him on the other side.

Then there came forth a Summons for Mr *Stand-fast* (This Mr *Stand-fast* was he that the rest of the Pilgrims found upon his Knees in the Inchanted Ground), for the Post brought it him open in his hands. The contents whereof

[2] From "The Pilgrim's Progress."

were, *that he must prepare for a Change of Life, for his Master was not willing that he should be so far from him any longer.* At this Mr *Standfast* was put into a muse. Nay, said the Messenger, you need not doubt of the truth of my Message, for here is a Token of the Truth thereof, *Thy Wheel is broken at the Cistern.* Then he called to him Mr *Great-heart* who was their Guide, and said unto him, Sir, altho it was not my hap to be much in your good Company in the days of my Pilgrimage, yet since the time I knew you, you have been profitable to me. When I came from home, I left behind me a Wife and five small Children, let me entreat you at your return (for I know that you will go and return to your Master's house, in hopes that you yet be a Conductor to more of the holy Pilgrims), that you send to my Family, and let them be acquainted with all that hath and shall happen unto me. Tell them moreover of my happy Arrival to this place, and of the present late blessed condition that I am in. Tell them also of *Christian* and *Christiana* his Wife, and how she and her Children came after her Husband. Tell them also of what a happy end she made and whither she is gone. I have little or nothing to send to my Family, except it be Prayers and Tears for them; of which it will suffice if thou acquaint them, if peradventure they may prevail.

When Mr *Stand-fast* had thus set things in order, and the time being come for him to haste him away, he also went down to the River. Now there was a great Calm at that time in the River; wherefore Mr *Stand-fast*, when he was about half-way in, he stood awhile, and talked to his Companions that had waited upon him thither. And he said,

This River has been a Terror to many, yea, the thoughts of it also have often frighted me. But now methinks I stand easy, my Foot is fixt upon that upon which the Feet of the Priests that bare the Ark of the Covenant stood while *Israel* went over this *Jordan*. The Waters indeed are to the Palate bitter and to the Stomach cold, yet the thoughts of what I am going to and of the Conduct that waits for me on the other side doth lie as a glowing Coal at my Heart.

I see myself now at the end of my Journey, my toilsome days are ended. I am going now to see that Head that was crowned with Thorns, and that Face that was spit upon for me.

I have formerly lived by Hear-say and Faith, but now I go where I shall live by sight, and shall be with Him in whose Company I delight myself.

I have loved to hear my Lord spoken of, and wherever I have seen the print of His Shoe in the Earth, there I have coveted to set my Foot too.

His name has been to me as a Civet-box, yea, sweeter than all Perfumes. His Voice to me has been most sweet, and his Countenance I have more desired than they that have most desired the Light of the Sun. His Word I did use to gather for my Food and for Antidotes against my Faintings. He has held me, and I have kept me from mine iniquities, yea, my Steps hath He strengthened in His Way.

Now while he was thus in Discourse, his Countenance changed, his strong man bowed under him, and after he had said, *Take me, for I come unto Thee,* he ceased to be seen of them.

But glorious it was to see how the open Region was filled with Horses and Chariots, with Trumpeters and Pipers, with Singers and Players on Stringed Instruments, to welcome the Pilgrims as they went up, and followed one another in at the beautiful Gate of the City.

III

ANCIENT VANITY FAIR[*]

THEN I saw in my Dream, that when they were got out of the Wilderness, they presently saw a Town before them, and the name of that Town is *Vanity;* and at the Town there is a Fair kept, called *Vanity Fair:* it is kept all the year long; it beareth the name of *Vanity Fair,* because the Town where 'tis kept *is lighter than Vanity;* and also because all that is there sold, or that cometh thither, is *Vanity.* As is the saying of the wise, *All that cometh is Vanity.*

This Fair is no new erected business, but a thing of ancient standing; I will shew you the original of it.

Almost five thousand years agone, there were Pilgrims walking to the Celestial City, as these two honest persons are; and *Beelzebub, Apollyon,* and *Legion,* with their Companions, perceiving by the path that the Pilgrims made, that their way to the city lay through this Town of *Vanity,*

[*] From "The Pilgrim's Progress."

they contrived here to set up a Fair; a Fair wherein should be sold of *all sorts of Vanity*, and that it should last all the year long: therefore at this Fair are all such Merchandise sold, as Houses, Lands, Trades, Places, Honors, Preferments, Titles, Countries, Kingdoms, Lusts, Pleasures, and Delights of all sorts, as Whores, Bawds, Wives, Husbands, Children, Masters, Servants, Lives, Blood, Bodies, Souls, Silver, Gold, Pearls, Precious Stones, and what not. . . .

Now, as I said, the way to the Celestial City lies just through this Town where this lusty Fair is kept; and he that will go to the City, and yet not go through this Town, must needs *go out of the World*. The Prince of Princes himself, when here, went through this Town to his own Country, and that upon a *Fair-day* too; yea, and as I think, it was *Beelzebub*, the chief Lord of this Fair, that invited him to buy of his Vanities: yea, would have made him Lord of the Fair, would he but have done him reverence as he went through the Town. Yea, because he was such a person of honor, *Beelzebub* had him from Street to Street, and shewed him all the Kingdoms of the World in a little time, that he might (if possible) allure that Blessed One to cheapen and buy some of his Vanities. But he had no mind to the Merchandise, and therefore left the Town, without laying out so much as one Farthing upon these Vanities. This Fair therefore is an ancient thing, of long standing, and a very great Fair. . . .

The Pilgrims being patient, and not rendering railing for railing, but contrarywise blessing, and giving good words for bad, and kindness for

injuries done, some men in the Fair that were
more observing, and less prejudiced than the
rest, began to check and blame the baser sort
for their continual abuses done by them to the
men; they therefore in angry manner let fly at
them again, counting them as bad as the men
in the Cage, and telling them that they seemed
confederates, and should be made partakers of
their misfortunes. The other replied, that for
ought they could see, the men were quiet, and
sober, and intended nobody any harm; and that
there were many that traded in their Fair that
were more worthy to be put into the Cage, yea,
and Pillory too, than were the men that they
had abused. Thus, after divers words had passed
on both sides (the men behaving themselves all
the while very wisely and soberly before them),
they fell to some blows among themselves, and
did harm one to another. Then were these two
poor men brought before their examiners again,
and there charged as being guilty of the late
hubbub that had been in the Fair. So they
beat them pitifully and hanged irons upon them,
and led them in chaines up and down the Fair,
for an example and a terror to others, lest any
should further speak in their behalf, or join
themselves unto them. But *Christian* and *Faithful* behaved themselves yet more wisely, and
received the ignominy and shame that was cast
upon them, with so much meekness and patience,
that it won to their side (tho but few in
comparison of the rest) several of the men in
the Fair. This put the other party yet into a
greater rage, insomuch that they concluded the
death of these two men. Wherefore they threat-

ened, that the Cage nor irons should serve their
turn, but that they should die, for the abuse they
had done, and for deluding the men of the Fair.

> Behold Vanity Fair; the Pilgrims there
> > Are chained and stoned beside;
> Even so it was, our Lord past here,
> > And on Mount Calvary died.

Then were they remanded to the Cage again,
until further order should be taken with them.
So they put them in, and made their feet fast
in the Stocks.

Here also they called again to mind what they
had heard from their faithful friend *Evangelist*,
and were the more confirmed in their way and
sufferings, by what he told them would happen
to them. They also now comforted each other,
that whose lot it was to suffer, even he should
have the best on't; therefore each man secretly
wished that he might have that preferment: but
committing themselves to the Allwise dispose
of Him that ruleth all things, with much content
they abode in the condition in which they were,
until they should be otherwise disposed of.

Then a convenient time being appointed, they
brought them forth to their Tryal, in order to
their condemnation. When the time was come,
they were brought before their enemies, and ar-
raigned. The Judge's name was Lord *Hate-good*.
Their Indictment was one and the same in substance, tho somewhat varying in form, the
contents whereof was this:

*That they were enemies to and disturbers of
their Trade; that they had made Commotions and*

Divisions in the Town, and had won a party to their own most dangerous Opinions in contempt of the Law of their Prince.

> Now *Faithful* play the Man, speak for thy God:
> Fear not the wickeds' malice, nor their rod:
> Speak boldly man, the Truth is on thy side;
> Die for it, and to Life in triumph ride.

Then *Faithful* began to answer, that he had only set himself against that which had set itself against Him that is higher than the highest. And said he, as for Disturbance, I make none, being myself a man of Peace; the Party that were won to us, were won by beholding our Truth and Innocence, and they are only turned from the worse to the better. And as to the King you talk of, since he is *Beelzebub*, the enemy of our Lord, I defy him and all his Angels.

Then Proclamation was made, that they that had aught to say for their Lord the King against the Prisoner at the Bar, should forthwith appear and give in their evidence. So there came in three witnesses, to wit, *Envy*, *Superstition*, and *Pickthank*. They were then asked if they knew the Prisoner at the Bar; and what they had to say for their Lord the King against him.

Then stood forth *Envy*, and said to this effect: My Lord, I have known this man a long time, and will attest upon my Oath before this honorable Bench, that he is—

Judge. Hold! Give him his Oath.

So they sware him.

Then he said, My Lord, this man, notwithstanding his plausible name, is one of the vilest

men in our Country. He neither regardeth
Prince nor People, Law nor Custom; but doth
all that he can to possess all men with certain
of his disloyal notions, which he in the general
calls Principles of Faith and Holiness. And in
particular, I heard him once myself affirm *That
Christianity and the Customs of our Town of
Vanity were diametrically opposite, and could not
be reconciled.* By which saying, my Lord, he
doth at once not only condemn all our laudable
doings, but us in the doing of them.

Judge. Then did the Judge say to him, Hast
thou any more to say?

Envy. My Lord, I could say much more, only
I would not be tedious to the Court. Yet if
need be, when the other Gentlemen have given
in their Evidence, rather than anything shall
be wanting that will despatch him, I will enlarge my Testimony against him.

So he was bid stand by. Then they called
Superstition, and bid him look upon the Prisoner.
They also asked, what he could say for their
Lord the King against him. Then they sware
him; so he began:

Super. My Lord, I have no great acquaintance
with this man, nor do I desire to have further
knowledge of him; however, this I know, that he
is a very pestilent fellow, from some discourse
that the other day I had with him in this
Town; for then talking with him, I heard him
say, That our Religion was naught, and such
by which a man could by no means please God.
Which sayings of his, my Lord, your Lordship
very well knows, what necessarily thence will
follow, to wit, That we still do worship in vain,

are yet in our sins, and finally shall be damned; and this is that which I have to say.

Then was *Pickthank* sworn, and bid say what he knew, in behalf of their Lord the King, against the prisoner at the Bar.

Pick. My Lord, and you, Gentlemen all, This fellow I have known of a long time, and have heard him speak things that ought not to be spoke; for he hath railed on our noble Prince *Beelzebub*, and hath spoken contemptibly of his honorable Friends, whose names are the Lord *Old Man*, the Lord *Carnal Delight*, the Lord *Luxurious*, the Lord *Desire of Vain Glory*, my old Lord *Lechery*, Sir *Having Greedy*, with all the rest of our Nobility; and he hath said moreover, That if all men were of his mind, if possible, there is not one of these Noblemen should have any longer a being in this Town; besides, he hath not been afraid to rail on you, my Lord, who are now appointed to be his Judge, calling you an ungodly villain, with many other suchlike vilifying terms, with which he hath bespattered most of the Gentry of our Town.

When this *Pickthank* had told his tale, the Judge directed his speech to the Prisoner at the Bar, saying, Thou Runagate, Heretick, and Traitor, hast thou heard what these honest Gentlemen have witnessed against thee?

Faith. May I speak a few words in my own defense?

Judge. Sirrah, sirrah, thou deservest to live no longer, but to be slain immediately upon the place; yet that all men may see our gentleness towards thee, let us see what thou hast to say.

Faith. 1. I say then, in answer to what Mr

Envy hath spoken, I never said ought but this, *That what Rule or Laws or Custom or People, were flat against the Word of God, are diametrically opposite to Christianity.* If I have said amiss in this, convince me of my error, and I am ready here before you to make my recantation.

2. As to the second, to wit, Mr *Superstition*, and his charge against me, I said only this, *That in the worship of God there is required a Divine Faith; but there can be no Divine Faith without a Divine Revelation of the will of God: therefore whatever is thrust into the Worship of God that is not agreeable to a Divine Revelation, cannot be done but by an human faith, which faith will not profit to Eternal Life.*

3. As to what Mr *Pickthank* hath said, I say (avoiding terms, as that I am said to rail, and the like) that the Prince of this Town, with all the rabblement his attendants, by this Gentleman named, are more fit for a being in Hell, than in this Town and Country: *and so, the Lord have mercy upon me.* . . . .

Then went the Jury out, whose names were, Mr *Blind-Man*, Mr *No-good*, Mr *Malice*, Mr *Love-lust*, Mr *Live-loose*, Mr *Heady*, Mr *Highmind*, Mr *Enmity*, Mr *Lyar*, Mr *Cruelty*, Mr *Hate-light*, and Mr *Implacable;* who every one gave in his private Verdict against him among themselves, and afterwards unanimously concluded to bring him in guilty before the Judge. And first among themselves, Mr *Blind-man* the Foreman, said, *I see clearly that this man is an Heretick.* Then said Mr *No-good, Away with such a fellow from the earth. Ay,* said Mr *Malice,*

for I hate the very looks of him. Then said Mr
Love-lust, I could never endure him. Nor I, said
Mr *Live-loose, for he would always be condemning
my way. Hang him, hang him,* said Mr *Heady.
A sorry Scrub,* said Mr *High-mind. My heart
riseth against him,* said Mr *Enmity. He is a
rogue,* said Mr *Lyar. Hanging is too good for
him,* said Mr *Cruelty. Let us dispatch him out
of the way,* said Mr *Hate-light.* Then said Mr
*Implacable, Might I have all the world given me,
I could not be reconciled to him; therefore let us
forthwith bring him in guilty of death.* And so
they did; therefore he was presently condemned
to be had from the place where he was, to the
place from whence he came, and there to be
put to the most cruel death that could be in-
vented.

They therefore brought him out, to do with
him according to their Law; and first they
Scourged him, then they Buffeted him, then they
Lanced his flesh with Knives; after that they
Stoned him with stones, then pricked him with
their Swords; and last of all they burned him
to ashes at the Stake. Thus came *Faithful* to
his end.

Brave *Faithful,* bravely done in Word and
  Deed;
Judge, Witnesses, and Jury have instead
Of overcoming thee, but shewn their Rage:
When thou art dead, thou'lt live from Age
  to Age.

JOHN DRYDEN

Born in 1631, died in 1700; educated at Cambridge; originally a Parliamentarian, but went over to the Royalists;
made poet-laureate in 1670; converted to Catholicism in
1686; his life written by Samuel Johnson; his works collected in 1808 in eighteen volumes by Sir Walter Scott.

OF ELIZABETHAN DRAMATISTS[1]

To begin, then, with Shakespeare. He was the
man who, of all modern, and perhaps ancient
poets, had the largest and most comprehensive
soul. All the images of nature were still present
to him, and he drew them not laboriously, but
luckily. When he describes anything, you more
than see it—you feel it too. Those who accused
him to have wanted learning, give him the greater
commendation. He was naturally learned; he
needed not the spectacles of books to read nature; he looked inwards, and found her there.
I cannot say he is everywhere alike; were he so,
I should do him injury to compare him with
the greatest of mankind. He is many times flat,
insipid; his comic wit degenerating into clenches,
his serious swelling into bombast. But he is
always great when some great occasion is presented to him; no man can say he ever had a
fit subject for his wit, and did not then raise
himself as high above the rest of poets.

Quantum lenta solent inter viburna cupressi.

The consideration of this made Mr. Hales of

[1] From the "Essay on Dramatic Poetry."

181

Eton[2] say, that there was no subject of which any poet ever writ, but he would produce it much better done in Shakespeare; and however others are now generally preferred before him, yet the age wherein he lived, which had contemporaries with him Fletcher and Jonson, never equalled them to him in their esteem. And in the last king's court, when Ben's reputation was at highest, Sir John Suckling, and with him the greater part of the courtiers, set our Shakespeare far above him. . . .

Beaumont and Fletcher, of whom I am next to speak, had with the advantage of Shakespeare's wit, which was their precedent, great natural gifts, improved by study; Beaumont especially, being so accurate a judge of plays, that Ben Jonson, while he lived, submitted all his writings to his censure, and 'tis thought, used his judgment in correcting, if not contriving, all his plots. What value he had for him, appears by the verses he writ to him, and therefore I need speak no farther of it. The first play that brought Fletcher and him in esteem was their "Philaster"; for before that they had written two or three very unsuccessfully: as the like is reported of Ben Jonson, before he writ "Every Man in his Humor." Their plots were generally more regular than Shakespeare's, especially those which were made before Beaumont's death; and they understood and imitated the conversation of gentlemen much better; whose wild debaucheries, and quickness of wit in repartees, no poet before

[2] John Hales, "the ever-memorable" canon of Windsor and author of "Golden Remains," born in 1584, died in 1656.

them could paint as they have done. Humor,
which Ben Jonson derived from particular persons, they made it not their business to describe;
they represented all the passions very lively, but
above all, love. I am apt to believe the English
language in them arrived to its highest perfection: what words have since been taken in, are
rather superfluous than ornamental. Their plays
are now the most pleasant and frequent entertainments of the stage; two of theirs being acted
through the year, for one of Shakespeare's or
Jonson's: the reason is, because there is a certain gaiety in their comedies, and pathos in their
more serious plays, which suits generally with
all men's humors. Shakespeare's language is likewise a little obsolete, and Ben Jonson's wit comes
short of theirs.

As for Jonson, to whose character I am now
arrived, if we look upon him while he was himself—for his last plays were but his dotages—
I think him the most learned and judicious
writer which any theater ever had. He was a
most severe judge of himself, as well as others.
One can not say he wanted wit, but rather that
he was frugal of it. In his works you find
little to retrench or alter. Wit, and language,
and humor also in some measure, we had before
him; but something of art was wanting to the
drama, till he came. He managed his strength
to more advantage than any who preceded him.
You seldom find him making love in any of his
scenes, or endeavoring to move the passions;
his genius was too sullen and saturnine to do
it gracefully, especially when he knew he came
after those who had performed both to such

a height. Humor was his proper sphere; and in that he delighted most to represent mechanic people. He was deeply conversant in the ancients, both Greek and Latin, and he borrowed boldly from them; there is scarce a poet or historian among the Roman authors of those times whom he has not translated in "Sejanus" and "Catiline." But he has done his robberies so openly that one may see he fears not to be taxed by any law. He invades authors like a monarch; and what would be theft in other poets, is only victory in him. With the spoils of these writers he so represents old Rome to us, in its rites, ceremonies, and customs, that if one of their poets had written either of his tragedies, we had seen less of it than in him.

If there was any fault in his language, 'twas that he weaved it too closely and laboriously, in his comedies especially: perhaps, too, he did a little too much Romanize our tongue, leaving the words which he translated almost as much Latin as he found them; wherein, tho he learnedly followed their language, he did not enough comply with the idiom of ours. If I would compare him with Shakespeare, I must acknowledge him the more correct poet, but Shakespeare the greater wit. Shakespeare was the Homer, or father of our dramatic poets: Jonson was the Virgil, the pattern of elaborate writing; I admire him, but I love Shakespeare. To conclude of him: as he has given us the most correct plays, so, in the precepts which he has laid down in his "Discoveries," we have as many and profitable rules for perfecting the stage, as any wherewith the French can furnish us.

SAMUEL PEPYS

Born in 1633, died in 1703; son of a London tailor; educated at Cambridge; a clerk in the Admiralty in 1660, becoming finally Secretary; conducted the entire administration during the great plague, when he alone remained in London; assisted in checking the great fire in 1666: elected to Parliament in 1678; President of the Royal Society in 1684-86; gave his library of three thousand volumes to one of the colleges at Cambridge; his "Diary," first published in 1825, was written in cipher, without intent of publication.

I

OF VARIOUS DOINGS OF MR. AND MRS. PEPYS[1]

August 18, 1660. — Towards Westminster by water. I landed my wife at Whitefriars with £5 to buy her a petticoat, and my father persuaded her to buy a most fine cloth, of 26s. a yard, and a rich lace, that the petticoat will come to £5; but she doing it very innocently, I could not be angry. Captain Ferrers took me and Creed to the Cockpit play, the first that I have had time to see since my coming from sea, *The Loyall Subject*, where one Kinaston, a boy, acted the Duke's sister, but made the loveliest lady that ever I saw in my life. After the play done, we went to drink, and, by Captain Ferrers' means, Kinaston, and another that acted Archas the General, came and drank with us.

19. (Lord's Day.)—This morning Sir W. Bat-

[1] From the "Diary."

ten, Pen, and myself, went to church to the churchwardens, to demand a pew, which at present could not be given us; but we are resolved to have one built. So we staid, and heard Mr. Mills, a very good minister. Home to dinner, where my wife had on her new petticoat that she bought yesterday, which indeed is a very fine cloth and a fine lace; but that being of a light color, and the lace all silver, it makes no great show.

March 2, 1667.—After dinner, with my wife, to the King's house to see *The Maiden Queene,* a new play of Dryden's mightily commended for the regularity of it, and the strain and wit; and, the truth is, there is a comical part done by Nell Gwynne, which is Florimell, that I never can hope ever to see the like done again, by man or woman. The King and Duke of York were at the play. But so great performance of a comical part was never, I believe, in the world before as Nell do this both as a mad girl, then most and best of all, when she comes in like a young gallant; and hath the motions and carriage of a spark the most that ever I saw any man have. It makes me, I confess, admire her.

October 5.—To the King's house; and there, going in, met with Knipp, and she took us up into the tireing-rooms: and to the woman's shift, where Nell was dressing herself, and was all unready, and is very pretty, prettier than I thought. And into the scene-room, and there sat down, and she gave us fruit: and here I read the questions to Knipp, while she answered me, through all her part of *Flora Figarys,* which was acted to-day. But, Lord! to see how they were both painted would make a man mad, and did make me loath them; and what base company of men comes among them, and how lewdly they talk! and how poor the men are in clothes, and yet what a show they make on the stage by candle-light, is very observable. But to see how Nell cursed for having so few people in the pit, was pretty; the other house carrying away all the people at the new play, and is said, now-a-days, to have generally most company, as being better players. By and by into the pit, and there saw the play, which is pretty good.

December 28.—To the King's house, and there saw *The Mad Couple*, which is but an ordinary play; but only Nell's and Hart's mad parts are most excellent done, but especially hers: which makes it a miracle to me to think how ill she do any serious part, as, the other day, just like a fool or changeling; and in a mad part do beyond imitation almost. It pleased us mightily to see the natural affection of a poor woman, the mother of one of the children, brought on the stage; the child crying, she by force got upon the stage, and took up her child, and carried it away off of the stage from Hart. Many fine faces here to-day.

February 27, 1667-8. — With my wife to the King's house, to see *The Virgin Martyr*, the first time it hath been acted a great while: and it is mighty pleasant; not that the play is worth much, but it is finely acted by Beck Marshall. But that which did please me beyond anything in the whole world was the wind-musick when the angel comes down, which is so sweet that it ravished me, and indeed, in a word, did wrap up my soul so that it made me really sick, just as I have formerly been when in love with my wife; that neither then, nor all the evening going home, and at home, I was able to think of anything, but remained all night transported, so as I could not believe that ever any musick hath that real command over the soul of a man as this did upon me: and makes me resolve to practise wind-musick, and to make my wife do the like.

May 26, 1667.—My wife and I to church, where several strangers of good condition come to our pew. After dinner, I by water alone to Westminster to the parish church, and there did entertain myself with my perspective glass up and down the church, by which I had the great pleasure of seeing and gazing at a great many very fine women; and what with that, and sleeping, I passed away the time till sermon was done. I away to my boat, and up with it as far as Barne Elmes, reading of Mr. Evelyn's late new book against Solitude, in which I do not find much excess of good matter, tho it be pretty for a bye discourse.

August 18.—To Cree Church, to see it how it is: but I find no alteration there, as they there was, for my Lord Mayor and Aldermen to come to sermon, as they do every Sunday, as they did formerly to Paul's. There dined with me Mr. Turner and his daughter Betty. Betty is grown a fine young lady as to carriage and discourse. We had a good haunch of venison, powdered and boiled, and a good dinner. I walked towards Whitehall, but, being wearied, turned into St. Dunstan's Church, where I heard an able sermon of the minister of the place; and stood by a pretty, modest maid, whom I did labor to take by the hand; but she would not, but got further and further from me; and, at last, I could perceive her to take pins out of her pocket to prick me if I should touch her again—which, seeing, I did forbear, and was glad I did spy her design. And then I fell to gaze upon another pretty maid, in a pew close to me, and she on me; and I did go about to take her by the hand, which she suffered a little and then withdrew. So the sermon ended.

May 11, 1667.—My wife being drest this day in fair hair did make me so mad, that I spoke not one word to her, tho I was ready to burst with anger. After that, Creed and I into the Park, and walked, a most pleasant evening, and so took coach, and took up my wife, and in my way home discovered my trouble to my wife for her white locks, swearing several times, which I pray God forgive me for, and bending my fist that I would not endure it. She, poor wretch, was surprised with it, and made me no answer all the way home; but there we parted, and I to the office late, and then home, and without supper to bed, vexed.

12. (Lord's Day.)—Up and to my chamber, to settle some accounts there, and by and by down comes my wife to me in her night-gown, and we begun calmly, that, upon having money to lace her gown for second mourning, she would promise to wear white locks no more in my sight, which I, like a severe fool, thinking not enough, begun to except against, and made her fly out to very high terms and cry, and in her heat, told me of

189

keeping company with Mrs. Knipp, saying, that if I would promise never to see her more—of whom she hath more reason to suspect than I had heretofore of Pembleton—she would never wear white locks more. This vexed me, but I restrained myself from saying anything, but do think never to see this woman—at least, to have her here more—and so all very good friends as ever. My wife and I bethought ourselves to go to a French house to dinner, and so inquired out Monsieur Robins, my perriwigg-maker, who keeps an ordinary, and in an ugly street in Covent Garden, did find him at the door, and so we in; and in a moment almost had the table covered, and clean glasses, and all in the French manner, and a mess of potage first, and then a piece of bœuf-a-la-mode, all exceeding well seasoned, and to our great liking; at least it would have been anywhere else but in this bad street, and in a perriwigg-maker's house; but to see the pleasant and ready attendance that we had, and all things so desirous to please, and ingenious in the people, did take me mightily. Our dinner cost us 6s.

November 30, 1668.—My wife, after dinner, went the first time abroad in her coach, calling on Roger Pepys, and visiting Mrs. Creed, and my cosen Turner. Thus ended this month with very good content, but most expenseful to my purse on things of pleasure, having furnished my wife's closet and the best chamber, and a coach and horses, that ever I knew in the world; and I am put into the greatest condition of outward state that ever I was in, or hoped ever to be, or desired.

December 2.—Abroad with my wife, the first time that ever I rode in my own coach, which do make my heart rejoice, and praise God and pray Him to bless it to me and continue it. So she and I to the King's playhouse, and there saw *The Usurper;* a pretty good play, in all but what is designed to resemble Cromwell and Hugh Peters, which is mighty silly. The play done, we to Whitehall; where my wife staid while I up to the Duchesse's and Queene's side, to speak with the Duke of York: and here saw all the ladies, and heard the silly discourse of the King, with his people about him.

April 11, 1669.—Thence to the Park, my wife and I; and here Sir W. Coventry did first see me and my wife in a coach of our own; and so did also this night the Duke of York, who did eye my wife mightily. But I begin to doubt that my being so much seen in my own coach at this time may be observed to my prejudice; but I must venture it now.

II

ENGLAND WITHOUT CROMWELL [1]

July 12, 1667.—Up betimes and to my chamber, there doing business, and by and by comes Greeting and begun a new month with him, and now to learn to set anything from the notes upon the flageolet, but Lord! to see how like a fool he goes about to give direction would make a man mad. I then out and by coach to White

[1] From the "Diary."

Hall and to the Treasury chamber, where did a little business, and thence to the Exchequer to Burges, about Tangier business, and so back again stepping into the Hall a little, and then homeward by coach, and he with me to the Excise Office, there to do a little business also, in the way he telling me that undoubtedly the peace is concluded; for he did stand where he did hear part of the discourse at the Council table, and there did hear the King argue for it.

Among other things that the spirits of the seamen were down, and the forces of our enemies are grown too great and many for us, and he would not have his subjects overprest, for he knew an Englishman would do as much as any man upon hopeful terms; but where he sees he is overprest, he despairs soon as any other; and besides that, they have already such a load of dejection upon them, that they will not be in temper a good while again. He heard my Lord Chancellor say to the King, "Sir," says he, "the whole world do complain publickly of treachery, that things have been managed falsely by some of his great ministers." "Sir," says he, "I am for your Majesty's falling into a speedy enquiry into the truth of it, and, where you meet with it, punish it. But, at the same time, consider what you have to do, and make use of your time for having a peace; for more money will not be given without much trouble, nor is it, I fear, to be had of the people, nor will a little do it to put us into condition of doing our business." But Sir H. Cholmly tells me he (the Chancellor) did say the other day at his table, "Treachery," says he; "I could wish we could prove there was anything of that in it; for that would imply some wit and thoughtfulness; but we are ruined merely by folly and neglect.'' And so Sir H. Cholmly tell me they did all argue for peace and so he do believe that the King hath agreed to the three points Mr. Coventry brought over, which I have mentioned before, and is gone with them back. . . .

While we were at the Excise Office talking with Mr. Ball, it was computed that the Parliament had given the King for this war only, besides all prizes, and besides the £200,000 which he was to spend of his own revenue to guard the sea, above £5,000,000 and odd £100,000; which is a most prodigious sum. Sir H. Cholmly, as a true English gentleman, do decry the King's expenses of his Privy-purse, which in King James's time did not rise to above £5,000 a year, and in King Charles's to £10,000, do now cost us above £100,-000 besides the great charge of the Monarchy, as the Duke of York £100,000 of it, and other limbs of the Royal family, and the guards, which, for his part, says he, ''I would have all disbanded, for the King is not the better by them, and would be as safe without them; for we have had no rebellions to make him fear anything.'' But contrarily, he is now raising of a land army, which this Parliament and Kingdom will never bear, besides, the commanders they put over them are such as will never be able to raise or command them; but the design is, and the Duke of York he says, is hot for it, to have a land army, and so to make the government like that of France, but our princes have not brains, or at least care and forecast enough to do that.

It is strange how he and everybody now-a-days do reflect upon Oliver,[2] and commend him, what brave things he did, and made all the neighbor princes fear him; while here a prince, come in with all the love and prayers and good liking of his people, who have given greater signs of his loyalty and willingness to serve him with their estates than ever was done by any other people, hath lost all so soon, that it is a miracle what way a man could devise to lose so much in so little time.

Thence he set me down at my Lord Crew's and away, and I up to my Lord, where Sir Thomas Crew was, and by and by comes Mr. Cæsar, who teaches my Lady's page upon the lute, and here Mr. Cæsar did play some very fine things indeed, to my great liking. Here was my Lord Hitchingbroke also, newly come from Hitchingbroke, where all well, but methinks I knowing in what case he stands for money by his demands to me and the report Mr. Moore gives of the management of the family, make me, God forgive me! to contemn him, tho I do really honor and pity them, tho they deserve it not that have so good an estate and will live beyond it. To dinner, and very good discourse with my Lord. And after dinner, Sir Thomas Crew and I alone, and he tells me how I am mightily in esteem with the Parliament; there being harangues made in the House to the Speaker, of Mr. Pepy's readiness and civility to shew them everything, which I am this time very glad of.

[2] Oliver Cromwell had died in 1658, nine years before the date of Pepy's paragraph.

GILBERT BURNET

Born in 1643, died in 1715; accompanied William III from Holland to England as chaplain in 1688; made Bishop of Salisbury in 1689; his "History of Our Own Times" published after his death in 1723-34, having been edited by his son; other works published in his lifetime.

CHARLES II[1]

THUS lived and died King Charles II. He was the greatest instance in history of the various revolutions of which any one man seemed capable, He was bred up the first twelve years of his life with the splendor that became the heir of so great a crown. After that, he passed through eighteen years of great inequalities; unhappy in the war, in the loss of his father, and of the crown of England. Scotland did not only receive him, tho upon terms hard of digestion, but made an attempt upon England for him, tho a feeble one. He lost the battle of Worcester with too much indifference. And then he shewed more care of his person than became one who had so much at stake. He wandered about England for ten weeks after that, hiding from place to place. But, under all the apprehensions he had then upon him, he shewed a temper so careless, and

[1] From the "History of Our Own Times."

so much turned to levity, that he was then diverting himself with little household sports, in as unconcerned a manner as if he had made no loss, and had been in no danger at all. He got at last out of England. But he had been obliged to so many who had been faithful to him, and careful of him, that he seemed afterwards to resolve to make an equal return to them all; and finding it not easy to reward them all as they deserved, he forgot them all alike. Most princes seem to have this pretty deep in them, and to think that they ought not to remember past services, but that their acceptance of them is a full reward. He, of all in our age, exerted this piece of prerogative in the amplest manner; for he never seemed to charge his memory, or to trouble his thoughts, with the sense of any of the services that had been done him.

While he was abroad at Paris, Cologne, or Brussels, he never seemed to lay anything to heart. He pursued all his diversions and irregular pleasures in a free career, and seemed to be as serene under the loss of a crown as the greatest philosopher could have been. Nor did he willingly hearken to any of those projects with which he often complained that his chancellor persecuted him. That in which he seemed most concerned was, to find money for supporting his expense. And it was often said, that if Cromwell would have compounded the matter, and have given him a good round pension, that he might have been induced to resign his title to him. During his exile, he delivered himself so entirely to his pleasures, that he became incapable of application. He spent little of his

time in reading or study, and yet less in thinking.
And in the state his affairs were then in, he accustomed himself to say to every person, and
upon all occasions, that which he thought would
please most; so that words or promises went very
easily from him. And he had so ill an opinion
of mankind, that he thought the great art of
living and governing was, to manage all things
and all persons with a depth of craft and dis-
simulation. And in that few men in the world
could put on the appearances of sincerity better
than he could; under which so much artifice was
usually hid, that in conclusion he could deceive
none, for all were become mistrustful of him.

He had great vices, but scarce any virtues to
correct them. He had in him some vices that
were less hurtful, which corrected his more hurtful ones. He was, during the active part of life,
given up to sloth and lewdness to such a degree,
that he hated business, and could not bear the
engaging in anything that gave him much trouble,
or put him under any constraint. And tho he
desired to become absolute, and to overturn both
our religion and our laws, yet he would neither
run the risk, nor give himself the trouble, which
so great a design required. He had an appearance of gentleness in his outward deportment;
but he seemed to have no bowels nor tenderness
in his nature, and in the end of his life he became
cruel. He was apt to forgive all crimes, even
blood itself, yet he never forgave anything that
was done against himself, after his first and general act of indemnity, which was to be reckoned
as done rather upon maxims of state than inclinations of mercy. He delivered himself up

to a most enormous course of vice, without any sort of restraint, even from the consideration of the nearest relations. The most studied extravagances that way seemed, to the very last, to be much delighted in and pursued by him. He had the art of making all people grow fond of him at first, by a softness in his whole way of conversation, as he was certainly the best-bred man of the age. But when it apeared how little could be built on his promise, they were cured of the fondness that he was apt to raise in them. When he saw young men of quality, who had something more than ordinary in them, he drew them about him, and set himself to corrupt them both in religion and morality; in which he proved so unhappily successful, that he left England much changed at his death from what he had found it at his restoration.

He loved to talk over all the stories of his life to every new man that came about him. His stay in Scotland, and the share he had in the war of Paris, in carrying messages from one side to the other, were his common topics. He went over these in a very graceful manner, but so often and so copiously, that all those who had been long accustomed to them grew weary of them; and when he entered on those stories, they usually withdrew: so that he often began them in a full audience, and before he had done, there were not above four or five persons left about him: which drew a severe jest from Wilmot, Earl of Rochester.[2] He said he wondered to see a

[2] The profligate earl, of whom the best-known anecdote is that he once pinned to the door of the King's chamber the following quatrain:

man have so good a memory as to repeat the same story without losing the least circumstance, and yet not remember that he had told it to the same persons the very day before. This made him fond of strangers, for they harkened to all his oft-repeated stories, and went away as in a rapture at such an uncommon condescension of a king.

His person and temper, his vices as well as his fortunes, resemble the character that we have given us of Tiberius so much, that it were easy to draw the parallel between them. Tiberius's banishment, and his coming afterward to reign, makes the comparison in that respect come pretty near. His hating of business, and his love of pleasures; his raising of favorites, and trusting them entirely; and his pulling them down, and hating them excessively; his art of covering deep designs, particularly of revenge, with an appearance of softness, brings them so near a likeness, that I did not wonder much to observe the resemblance of their faces and persons. At Rome, I saw one of the last statues made for Tiberius, after he had lost his teeth. But, bating the alteration which that made, it was so like King Charles, that Prince Borghese and Signior Dominico, to whom it belonged, did agree with me in thinking that it looked like a statute made for him.

> "Here lies our Sovereign Lord the King,
>   Whose word no man relies on;
> He never said a foolish thing,
>   And never did a wise one."

It is recorded of the King that, when he saw these lines he remarked that they were quite true, inasmuch as his words were his own and his acts were those of his ministers.

Few things ever went near his heart. The Duke of Gloucester's death seemed to touch him much. But those who knew him best, thought it was because he had lost him by whom only he could have balanced the surviving brother, whom he hated, and yet embroiled all his affairs to preserve the succession to him. . . .

No part of his character looked wickeder, as well as meaner, than that he, all the while that he was professing to be of the Church of England, expressing both zeal and affection to it, was yet secretly reconciled to the Church of Rome; thus mocking God, and deceiving the world with so gross a prevarication. And his not having the honesty or courage to own it at the last; his not shewing any sign of the least remorse for his ill-led life, or any tenderness either for his subjects in general, or for the queen and his servants; and his recommending only his mistresses and their children to his brother's care, would have been a strange conclusion to any other's life, but was well enough suited to all the other parts of his.

DANIEL DEFOE

Born in 1661, died in 1731; his father a butcher in London; served in the army in 1688; traveled on the Continent; wrote pamphlets in favor of William III; arrested and placed in the pillory for an attack on Dissenters in 1703; engaged in political intrigues and wrote many articles and pamphlets; "Robinson Crusoe" published in 1719, "Moll Flanders" in 1722, "The Journal of the Plague" in 1722.

I

THE SHIPWRECK OF CRUSOE[1]

NOTHING can describe the confusion of thought which I felt when I sunk into the water; for tho I swam very well, yet I could not deliver myself from the waves so as to draw my breath; till that wave having driven me or rather carried me a vast way on toward the shore, and having spent itself, went back, and left me upon the land almost dry, but half dead with the water I took in. I had so much presence of mind as well as breath left, that seeing myself nearer the mainland than I expected, I got upon my feet, and endeavored to make on toward the land as I could, before another wave should return and take me up again; but I soon found it was impossible to avoid it; for I saw the sea coming after me as high as a great hill, and as furious as an enemy which I had no means or strength

[1] From "The Life and Surprizing Adventures of Robinson Crusoe."

to contend with: my business was to hold my breath, and raise myself upon the water, if I could; and so by swimming to preserve my breathing, and pilot myself toward the shore if possible; my greatest concern now being that the wave, as it would carry me a great way toward the shore when it came on, might not carry me back again with it when it gave back toward the sea.

The wave that came upon me again buried me at once twenty or thirty feet deep in its own body; and I could feel myself carried with a mighty force and swiftness toward the shore, a very great way; but I held my breath, and assisted myself to swim still forward with all my might. I was ready to burst with holding my breath, when, as I felt myself rising up, so to my immediate relief I found my head and hands shoot out above the surface of the water; and tho it was not two seconds of time that I could keep myself so, yet it relieved me greatly, gave me breath and new courage. I was covered again with water a good while, but not so long but I held it out; and finding the water had spent itself, and began to return, I struck forward against the return of the waves, and felt ground again with my feet. I stood still a few moments to recover breath, and till the water went from me, and then took to my heels and ran with what strength I had farther toward the shore. But neither would this deliver me from the fury of the sea, which came pouring in after me again; and twice more I was lifted up by the waves and carried forward as before, the shore being very flat.

The last time of these two had well-nigh been fatal to me; for the sea having hurried me along as before, landed me, or rather dashed me against a piece of rock, and that with such force that it left me senseless, and indeed helpless as to my own deliverance; for the blow taking my side and breast, beat the breath as it were quite out of my body, and had it returned again immediately I must have been strangled in the water; but I recovered a little before the return of the waves, and seeing I should again be covered with the water, I resolved to hold fast by a piece of the rock, and so to hold my breath if possible till the wave went back. Now, as the waves were not so high as the first, being nearer land, I held my hold till the wave abated, and then fetched another run, which brought me so near the shore that the next wave, tho it went over me, yet did not so swallow me up as to carry me away; and the next run I took, I got to the mainland, where to my great comfort I clambered up the cliffs of the shore, and sat me down upon the grass, free from danger and quite out of the reach of the water.

I was now landed, and safe on shore; and began to look up and thank God that my life was saved, in a case wherein there were, some minutes before, scarce any room to hope. I believe it is impossible to express, to the life, what the ecstasies and transports of the soul are when it is so saved, as I may say, out of the grave: and I did not wonder now at the custom, viz., that when a malefactor who has the halter about his neck is tied up, and just going to be turned off, and has a reprieve brought to him—I say I do not wonder that they bring a surgeon with it, to let him blood that very moment they tell him of it; that the surprize may not drive the animal spirits from the heart and overwhelm him.

"For sudden joys, like griefs, confound at first."

I walked about the shore, lifting up my hands, and my whole being, as I may say, wrapt up in the contemplation of my deliverance; making a thousand gestures and motions which I can not describe; reflecting upon my comrades that were drowned, and that there should not be one soul saved but myself; for as for them, I never saw them afterward, or any sign of them, except three of the hats, one cap, and two shoes that were not fellows.

II

THE RESCUE OF MAN FRIDAY [*]

ABOUT a year and a half after I entertained these notions (and by long musing had, as it were, resolved them all into nothing, for want of an occasion to put them in execution), I was surprized one morning early by seeing no less than five canoes all on shore together on my side the island, and the people who belonged to them all landed and out of my sight. The number of them broke all my measures; for seeing so many,

[*] From "The Life and Surprizing Adventures of Robinson Crusoe."

and knowing that they always came four or six, or sometimes more, in a boat, I could not tell what to think of it, or how to take my measures to attack twenty or thirty men single-handed; so lay still in my castle, perplexed and discomforted. However, I put myself into all the same postures for an attack that I had formerly provided, and was just ready for action, if anything had presented. Having waited a good while, listening to hear if they made any noise, at length, being very impatient, I set my guns at the foot of my ladder, and clambered up to the top of the hill, by my two stages, as usual; standing so, however, that my head did not appear above the hill, so that they could not perceive me by any means. Here I observed, by the help of my perspective glass, that they were no less than thirty in number; that they had a fire kindled, and that they had meat drest. How they had cooked it, I knew not, or what it was; but they were all dancing, in I know not how many barbarous gestures and figures, their own way, round the fire.

While I was thus looking on them, I perceived, by my perspective, two miserable wretches dragged from the boats, where, it seems, they were laid by, and were now brought out for the slaughter. I perceived one of them immediately fall; being knocked down, I suppose with a club or wooden sword, for that was their way; and two or three others were at work immediately, cutting him open for their cookery, while the other victim was left standing by himself, till they should be ready for him. In that very moment, this poor wretch, seeing himself a little at liberty,

shot. The poor savage who fled, but had stopt,
tho he saw both his enemies fallen and killed,
as he thought, yet was so frightened with the
fire and noise of my piece that he stood stock
still, and neither came forward nor went backward, tho he seemed rather inclined still to fly
than to come on. I hallooed again to him, and
made signs to come forward, which he easily
understood, and came a little way; then stopt
again, and then a little farther, and stopt again;
and I could then perceive that he stood trem-
bling, as if he had been taken prisoner, and had
just been to be killed, as his two enemies were.
I beckoned to him again to come to me, and
gave him all the signs of encouragement that I
could think of; and he came nearer and nearer,
kneeling down every ten or twelve steps, in token
of acknowledgment for saving his life. I smiled
at him, and looked pleasantly, and beckoned to
him to come still nearer; at length, he came close
to me; and then he kneeled down again, kissed
the ground, and laid his head upon the ground,
and, taking me by the foot, set my foot upon his
head; this, it seems, was in token of swearing
to be my slave forever. I took him up, and
made much of him, and encouraged him all I
could.

But there was more work to do yet; for I
perceived the savage whom I had knocked down
was not killed, but stunned with the blow, and
began to come to himself. So I pointed to him,
and showed him the savage, that he was not
dead; upon this he spoke some words to me, and
tho I could not understand them, yet I thought
they were pleasant to hear; for they were the

first sound of a man's voice that I had heard, my own excepted, for above twenty-five years. But there was no time for such reflections now; the savage who was knocked down recovered himself so far as to sit up upon the ground, and I perceived that my savage began to be afraid; but when I saw that, I presented my other piece at the man, as if I would shoot him; upon this my savage, for so I call him now, made a motion to me to lend him my sword, which hung naked in a belt by my side, which I did. He no sooner had it, but he runs to his enemy, and at one blow cut off his head as cleverly, no executioner in Germany could have done it sooner or better; which I thought very strange for one who, I had reason to believe, never saw a sword in his life before, except their own wooden swords: however, it seems, as learned afterwards, they make their wooden swords so sharp, so heavy, and the wood is so hard, that they will even cut off heads with them, ay, and arms, and that at one blow too. When he had done this, he comes laughing to me in sign of triumph, and brought me the sword again, and with abundance of gestures which I did not understand, laid it down, with the head of the savage that he had killed just before me. But that which astonished him most, was to know how I killed the other Indian so far off; so pointing to him, he made signs to me to let him go to him; and I bade him go, as well as I could. When he came to him, he stood like one amazed, looking at him, turning him first on one side, then on the other; looked at the wound the bullet had made, which it seems was just in his breast, where it had made a hole, and no great quantity of blood had followed; but he had bled inwardly, for he was quite dead.

Upon this he made signs to me that he should bury them with sand, that they might not be seen by the rest, if they followed; and so I made signs to him again to do so. He fell to work; and in an instant he had scraped a hole in the sand with his hands, big enough to bury the first in, and then dragged him into it, and covered him; and did so by the other also; I believe he had buried them both in a quarter of an hour. Then calling him away, I carried him, not to my castle, but quite away to my cave, on the farther part of the island; so I did not let my dream come to pass in that part, that he came into my grove for shelter. Here I gave him bread and a bunch of raisins to eat, and a draft of water, which I found he was indeed in great distress for from his running; and having refreshed him, I made signs for him to go and lie down to sleep, showing him a place where I had laid some rice straw, and a blanket upon it, which I used to sleep upon myself sometimes; so the poor creature lay down, and went to sleep.

III

IN THE TIME OF THE GREAT PLAGUE*

A BLAZING star or comet appeared for several
months before the plague, as there did the year
after, another, a little before the fire; the old
women, and the phlegmatic hypochondriac part
of the other sex, whom I could almost call the
old women too, remarked, especially afterward,
tho not till both those judgments were over, that
those two comets passed directly over the city,
and that so very near the houses that it was
plain they imported something peculiar to the
city alone. That the comet before the pestilence
was of a faint, dull, languid color, and its motion
very heavy, solemn, and slow; but that the comet
before the fire was bright and sparkling, or as
others said, flaming, and its motion swift and
furious; and that accordingly one foretold a
heavy judgment, slow but severe, terrible, and
frightful, as was the plague. But the other foretold a stroke, sudden, swift, and fiery, as was the
conflagration; nay, so particular some people
were, that as they looked upon that comet pre-
ceding the fire they fancied that they not only
saw it pass swiftly and fiercely, and could perceive the motion with their eye, but they even
heard it—that it made a rushing mighty noise,
fierce and terrible, tho at a distance and but
just perceivable.

*From the "History of the Great Plague in London."
The year of the plague was 1665.

The shutting up of houses was at first counted a very cruel and unchristian method, and the poor people so confined made bitter lamentations; complaints of the severity of it were also daily brought to my lord mayor, of houses causelessly and some maliciously shut up; I can not say, but upon inquiry, many that complained so loudly were found in a condition to be continued; and others again, inspection being made upon the sick person and the sickness not appearing infectious, or if uncertain, yet on his being content to be carried to the pest-house, was released.

As I went along Houndsditch one morning about eight o'clock there was a great noise; it is true indeed that there was not much crowd, because the people were not free to gather together, or to stay together when they were there, nor did I stay long there; but the outcry was loud enough to prompt my curiosity, and I called to one who looked out of a window, and asked what was the matter.

A watchman, it seems, had been employed to keep his post at the door of a house which was infected, or said to be infected, and was shut up; he had been there all night for two nights together, as he told his story, and the day watchman had been there one day, and was now come to relieve him; all this while no noise had been heard in the house, no light had been seen, they called for nothing, sent him on no errands, which used to be the chief business of the watchman, neither had they given him any disturbance, as he said from Monday afternoon, when he heard a great crying and screaming in the house, which as he supposed was occasioned by some of the family dying just at that time. It seems the night before, the dead-cart, as it was called, had been stopt there, and a servant-maid had been brought down to the door dead, and the buriers or bearers, as they were called, put her into the cart, wrapt only in a green rug, and carried her away.

The watchman had knocked at the door, it seems, when he heard that noise and crying as above, and nobody answered a great while; but at last one looked out and said with an angry quick tone, and yet a kind of crying voice, or a voice of one that was crying, "What d'ye want, that you make such a knocking?" He answered, "I am the watchman; how do you do? What is the matter?" The person answered, "What is that to you? Stop the dead-cart." This, it seems, was about one o'clock; soon after, as the fellow said, he stopt the dead-cart, and then knocked again, but nobody answered; he continued knocking, and the bellman called out several times, "Bring out your dead"; but nobody answered, till the man that drove the cart, being called to other houses, would stay no longer, and drove away.

The watchman knew not what to make of all this, so he let them alone till the morning man, or day watchman, as they called him, came to relieve him. Giving him an account of the particulars, they knocked at the door a great while, but nobody answered, and they observed that the window or casement at which the person looked out who had answered before, continued open, being up two pair of stairs.

Upon this the two men, to satisfy their curiosity, got a long ladder, and one of them went up to the window and looked into the room, where he saw a woman lying dead upon the floor in a dismal manner, having no clothes on but her shift; but tho he called aloud, and putting in his long staff, knocked hard on the floor, yet nobody stirred or answered; neither could he hear any noise in the house.

He came down upon this and acquainted his fellow, who went up also, and finding it just so, they resolved to acquaint either the lord mayor or some other magistrate of it, but did not offer to go in at the window. The magistrate, it seems, upon the information of the two men ordered the house to be broken open, a constable and other persons being appointed to be present, that nothing might be plundered; and accordingly it was so done, when nobody was found in the house but that young woman, who having been infected and past recovery, the rest had left her to die by herself, and every one gone, having found some way to delude the watchman and to get open the door, or get out at some back door, or over the tops of the houses, so that he knew nothing of it; and as to those cries and shrieks which he heard, it was supposed they were the passionate cries of the family at this bitter parting, which to be sure it was to them all, this being the sister to the mistress of the family. The man of the house, his wife, several children and servants, being all gone and fled; whether sick or sound, that I could never learn, nor indeed did I make much inquiry after it. . . .

This [38,195 deaths in about a month] was a

prodigious number of itself; but if I should add the reasons which I have to believe that this account was deficient, and how deficient it was, you would with me make no scruple to believe that there died above 10,000 a week for all those weeks, and a proportion for several weeks both before and after. The confusion among the people, especially within the city, at that time was inexpressible; the terror was so great at last that the courage of the people appointed to carry away the dead began to fail them; nay, several of them died, altho they had the distemper before, and were recovered; and some of them had dropt down when they had been carrying the bodies even at the pitside, and just ready to throw them in; and this confusion was greater in the city, because they had flattered themselves with hopes of escaping, and thought the bitterness of death was past. One cart, they told us, going up to Shoreditch, was forsaken by the drivers, or being left to one man to drive, he died in the street; and the horses, going on, overthrew the cart and left the bodies, some thrown here, some there, is a dismal manner. Another cart was, it seems, found in the great pit in Finsbury Fields, the driver being dead, or having been gone and abandoned it; and the horses running too near it, the cart fell in and drew the horses in also. It was suggested that the driver was thrown in with it and that the cart fell upon him, by reason his whip was seen to be in the pit among the bodies; but that, I suppose, could not be certain.

JONATHAN SWIFT

Born in 1667, died in 1745; educated at Trinity College,
Dublin; became secretary to Sir William Temple in 1688;
held small livings in Ireland in 1700 and other years;
lived mostly in London from 1701 to 1710, when he abandoned the Whigs and became a Tory; appointed by Queen
Anne dean of St. Patrick's, Dublin, in 1713; intimate with
Bolingbroke, Addison, Steele and Pope; published "Gulliver's Travels" in 1726; his mind clouded in later years,
and in 1741 he was put under restraint.

I

ON PRETENSE IN PHILOSOPHERS[1]

I WAS received very kindly by the warden, and
went for many days to the academy. Every room
hath in it one or more projectors, and I believe
I could not be in fewer than five hundred rooms.

The first man I saw was of a meager aspect,
with sooty hands and face, his hair and beard
long, ragged, and singed in several places. His
clothes, shirt, and skin were all of the same color.
He had been eight years upon a project for ex-
tracting sunbeams out of cucumbers, which were
to be put into phials hermetically sealed, and let
out to warm the air in raw inclement summers.
He told me he did not doubt in eight years more
that he should be able to supply the governor's
gardens with sunshine at a reasonable rate;
but he complained that his stock was low,

[1] From the description of the Academy of Lagado in
"Gulliver's Travels."

216

and entreated me to give him something as an encouragement to ingenuity, especially since this had been a very dear season for cucumbers. I made him a small present, for my lord had furnished me with money on purpose, because he knew their practise of begging from all who go to see them.

I saw another at work to calcine ice into gunpowder, who likewise shewed me a treatise he had written concerning the malleability of fire, which he intended to publish.

There was a most ingenious architect, who had contrived a new method for building houses, by beginning at the roof, and working downwards to the foundation; which he justified to me by the like practise of those two prudent insects, the bee and the spider.

There was an astronomer who had undertaken to place a sun-dial upon the great weather-cock on the town-house, by adjusting the annual and diurnal motions of the earth and sun, so as to answer and coincide with all accidental turning of the winds.

We crossed a walk to the other part of the academy, where, as I have already said, the projectors in speculative learning resided.

The first professor I saw was in a very large room, with forty pupils about him. After salutation, observing me to look earnestly upon a frame which took up the greatest part of both the length and breadth of the room, he said, perhaps I might wonder to see him employed in a project for improving speculative knowledge by practical and mechanical operations. But the world would soon be sensible of its usefulness, and he flattered himself that a more noble, exalted thought never sprang in any other man's head. Every one knew how laborious the usual method is of attaining to arts and sciences; whereas by his contrivance, the most ignorant person, at a reasonable charge, and with a little bodily labor, may write books in philosophy, poetry, politics, law, mathematics, and theology, without the least assistance from genius or study. He then led me to the frame, about the sides whereof all his pupils stood in ranks. It was twenty feet square, placed in the middle of the room. The superficies was composed of several bits of wood, about the bigness of a die, but some larger than others. They were all linked together by slender wires. These bits of wood were covered on every square with paper pasted on them; and on these papers were written all the words of their language in their several moods, tenses, and declensions, but without any order. The professor then desired me to observe, for he was going to set his engine at work. The pupils, at his command, took each of them hold of an iron handle, whereof there were forty fixt round the edges of the frame, and giving them a sudden turn, the whole disposition of the words was entirely changed. He then commanded six-and-thirty of the lads to read the several lines softly as they appeared upon the frame; and where they found three or four words together that might make part of a sentence, they dictated to the four remaining boys, who were scribes. This work was repeated three or four times, and at every turn the engine was so contrived that the words shifted into new places as the square bits of wood moved upside down. Six hours a day the young students were employed in this labor; and the professor shewed me several volumes in large folio, already collected of broken sentences, which he intended to piece together, and out of those rich materials give the world a complete body of all arts and sciences.

We next went to the school of languages, where three professors sat in consultation upon improving that of their own country.

The first project was to shorten discourse by cutting polysyllables into one, and leaving out verbs and participles; because, in reality, all things imaginable are but nouns. The other was a scheme for entirely abolishing all words whatsoever; and this was urged as a great advantage in point of health as well as brevity; for, it is plain that every word we speak is in some degree a diminution of our lungs by corrosion, and consequently contributes to the shortening of our lives. An expedient was therefore offered, that since words are only names for things, it would be more convenient for all men to carry about them such things as were necessary to express the particular business they are to discourse on. And this invention would certainly have taken place, to the great ease as well as health of the subject, if the women, in conjunction with the vulgar and illiterate, had not threatened to raise a rebellion, unless they might be allowed the liberty to speak with their tongues, after the manner of their forefathers; such constant irreconcilable enemies to science are the common people.

Another great advantage proposed by this invention was, that it would serve as a universal language to be understood in all civilized nations, whose goods and utensils are generally of the same kind, or nearly resembling, so that their uses might easily be comprehended. And thus ambassadors would be qualified to treat with foreign princes or ministers of state, to whose tongues they were utter strangers.

I was at the mathematical school, where the master taught his pupils after a method scarce imaginable to us in Europe. The proposition and demonstration were fairly written on a thin wafer, with ink composed of a cephalic tincture. This the student was to swallow upon a fasting stomach, and for three days following eat nothing but bread and water. As the wafer digested, the tincture mounted to his brain, bearing the proposition along with it. But the success hath not hitherto been answerable, partly by some error in the quantum or composition, and partly by the perverseness of lads, to whom this bolus is so nauseous that they generally steal aside, and discharge it upward before it can operate; neither have they been yet persuaded to use so long an abstinence as the prescription requires.

In the school of political projectors I was but ill entertained, the professors appearing in my judgment wholly out of their senses, which is a scene that never fails to make me melancholy. These unhappy people were proposing schemes for persuading monarchs to choose favorites upon the score of their wisdom, capacity and virtue; of teaching ministers to consult the public good; of rewarding merit, great abilities, and eminent services; of instructing princes to know their true interest, by placing it on the same foundation with that of their people; of choosing for employments persons qualified to exercise them; with many other wild impossible chimeras that never entered before into the heart of man to conceive, and confirmed in me the old observation, that there is nothing so extravagant and irrational which some philosophers have not maintained for truth.

II

ON THE HOSPITALITY OF THE VULGAR[1]

THOSE inferior duties of life which the French call *les petites morales*, or the smaller morals, are with us distinguished by the name of good manners or breeding. This I look upon, in the general notion of it, to be a sort of artificial good sense, adapted to the meanest capacities, and introduced to make mankind easy in their commerce with each other. Low and little understandings, without some rules of this kind, would be perpetually wandering into a thousand indecencies and irregularities in behavior; and in their ordinary conversation, fall into the same boisterous familiarities that one observeth amongst them when a debauch hath quite taken away the use of their reason. In other instances, it is odd to consider, that for want of common discretion, the very end of good breeding is wholly perverted; and civility, intended to make

[1] From No. 1 of "The Tatler."

us easy, is employed in laying chains and fetters upon us, in debarring us of our wishes, and in crossing our most reasonable desires and inclinations.

This abuse reigneth chiefly in the country, as I found to my vexation, when I was last there, in a visit I made to a neighbor about two miles from my cousin. As soon as I entered the parlor, they put me into the great chair that stood close by a huge fire, and kept me there by force until I was almost stifled. Then a boy came in great hurry to pull off my boots, which I in vain opposed, urging that I must return soon after dinner. In the meantime, the good lady whispered her eldest daughter, and slipt a key into her hand. The girl returned instantly with a beer-glass half full of *aqua mirabilis* and syrup of gillyflowers. I took as much as I had a mind for; but madam vowed I should drink it off—for she was sure it would do me good, after coming out of the cold air—and I was forced to obey; which absolutely took away my stomach. When dinner came in, I had a mind to sit at a distance from the fire; but they told me it was as much as my life was worth, and set me with my back just against it. Altho my appetite was quite gone, I resolved to force down as much as I could; and desired the leg of a pullet. "Indeed, Mr. Bickerstaff," says the lady, "you must eat a wing to oblige me"; and so put a couple upon my plate. I was persecuted at this rate during the whole meal. As often as I called for small beer, the master tipped the wink, and the servant brought me a brimmer of October. Some time after dinner, I ordered my cousin's man, who came with me, to get ready the horses, but it was resolved I should not stir that night; and when I seemed pretty much bent upon going, they ordered the stable door to be locked; and the children hid my cloak and boots. The next question was, what I would have for supper. I said I never ate anything at night; but was at last, in my own defense, obliged to name the first thing that came into my head. After three hours spent chiefly in apologies for my entertainment, insinuating to me, "that this was the worst time of the year for provisions; that they were at a great distance from any market; that they were afraid I should be starved; and that they knew they kept me to my loss," the lady went and left me to her husband—for they took special care I should never be alone. As soon as her back was turned, the little misses ran backward and forward every moment; and constantly as they came in or went out, made a courtesy directly at me, which in good manners I was forced to return with a bow, and, "Your humble servant, pretty miss." Exactly at eight the mother came up, and discovered by the redness of her face that supper was not far off.

It was twice as large as the dinner, and my persecution doubled in proportion. I desired at my usual hour to go to my repose, and was conducted to my chamber by the gentleman, his lady, and the whole train of children. They importuned me to drink something before I went to bed; and upon my refusing, at last left a bottle of *stingo*, as they called it, for fear I should wake and be thirsty in the night. I was forced in the morning to rise and dress myself in the dark, because they would not suffer my kinsman's servant to disturb me at the hour I desired to be called. I was now resolved to break through all measures to get away; and after sitting down to a monstrous breakfast of cold beef, mutton, neats'-tongues, venison-pasty, and stale beer, took leave of the family. But the gentleman would needs see me part of my way, and carry me a short-cut through his own grounds, which he told me would save half a mile's riding. This last piece of civility had like to have cost me dear, being once or twice in danger of my neck, by leaping over his ditches, and at last forced to alight in the dirt; when my horse, having slipt his bridle, ran away and took us up more than an hour to recover him again. It is evident that none of the absurdities I met with in this visit proceeded from an ill intention, but from a wrong judgment of complaisance, and a mis-application in the rules of it.

III

THE ART OF LYING IN POLITICS*

I AM prevailed on, through the importunity of friends, to interrupt the scheme I had begun in my last paper, by an essay upon the Art of Political Lying. We are told the devil is the father of lies, and was a liar from the beginning; so that, beyond contradiction, the invention is

*From "The Examiner."

old: and, which is more, his first essay of it was purely political, employed in undermining the authority of his prince, and seducing a third part of the subjects from their obedience: for which he was driven down from heaven, where (as Milton expresses it) he had been viceroy of a great western province; and forced to exercise his talent in inferior regions among other fallen spirits, poor or deluded men, whom he still daily tempts to his own sin, and will ever do so, till he be chained in the bottomless pit.

But altho the devil be the father of lies, he seems, like other great inventors, to have lost much of his reputation, by the continual improvements that have been made upon him.

Who first reduced lying into an art, and adapted it to politics, is not so clear from history, altho I have made some diligent inquiries. I shall therefore consider it only according to the modern system, as it has been cultivated these twenty years past in the southern part of our own island.

The poets tell us, that after the giants were overthrown by the gods, the earth in revenge produced her last offspring, which was Fame. And the fable is thus interpreted: that when tumults and seditions are quieted, rumors and false reports are plentifully spread through a nation. So that, by this account, lying is the last relief of a routed, earth-born, rebellious party in a state. But here the Moderns have made great additions, applying this art to the gaining of power and preserving it, as well as revenging themselves after they have lost it; as the same instruments are made use of by animals to feed themselves when they are hungry, and to bite those that tread upon them.

But the same genealogy can not always be admitted for political lying; I shall therefore desire to refine upon it, by adding some circumstances of its birth and parents. A political lie is sometimes born out of a discarded statesman's head, and thence delivered to be nursed and dandled by the rabble. Sometimes it is produced a monster, and licked into shape; at other times it comes into the world completely formed, and is spoiled in the licking. It is often born an infant in the regular way, and requires time to mature it; and often it sees the light in its full growth, but dwindles away by degrees. Sometimes it is of noble birth; and sometimes the spawn of a stockjobber. Here it screams aloud at the opening of the womb; and there it is delivered with a whisper. I know a lie that now disturbs half the kingdom with its noise, which, altho too proud and great at present to own its parents, I can remember its whisperhood. To conclude the nativity of this monster; when it comes into the world without a sting, it is stillborn; and whenever it loses its sting, it dies.

No wonder if an infant so miraculous in its birth should be destined for great adventures; and accordingly we see it hath been the guardian spirit of a prevailing party for almost twenty years. It can conquer kingdoms without fighting, and sometimes with the loss of a battle. It gives and resumes employments; can sink a mountain to a molehill, and raise a molehill to a mountain; hath presided for many years at committees of elections; can wash a blackamoor white; make a saint of an atheist, and a patriot of a profligate; can furnish foreign ministers with intelligence and raise or let fall the credit of the nation. This goddess flies with a huge looking-glass in her hands, to dazzle the crowd, and make them see, according as she turns it, their ruin in their interest, and their interest in their ruin. In this glass you will behold your best friends, clad in coats powdered with fleurs-de-lis, and triple crowns; their girdles hung round with chains, and beads, and wooden shoes; and your worst enemies adorned with the ensigns of liberty, property, indulgence, moderation, and a cornucopia in their hands. Her large wings, like those of a flying fish, are of no use but while they are moist; she therefore dips them in mud, and soaring aloft scatters it in the eyes of the multitude, flying with great swiftness; but at every turn is forced to stoop in dirty ways for new supplies.

I have been sometimes thinking, if a man had the art of the second sight for seeing lies, as they have in Scotland for seeing spirits, how admirably he might entertain himself in this town by observing the different shapes, sizes, and colors of those swarms of lies which buzz about the heads of some people, like flies about a horses' ears in summer; or those legions hovering every afternoon in Exchange alley, enough to darken the air; or over a club of discontented grandees, and thence sent down in cargoes to be scattered at elections.

IV

A MEDITATION UPON A BROOMSTICK[*]

THIS single stick, which you now behold ingloriously lying in that neglected corner, I once knew in a flourishing state in a forest. It was full of sap, full of leaves, and full of boughs; but now in vain does the busy art of man pretend to vie with nature, by tying that withered bundle of twigs to its sapless trunk; it is now at best but the reverse of what it was, a tree turned upside down, the branches on the earth, and the root in the air; it is now handled by every dirty wench, condemned to do her drudgery, and, by a capricious kind of fate, destined to make other things clean, and be nasty itself; at length, worn to the stumps in the service of the maids, it is either thrown out-of-doors, or condemned to the last use of kindling a fire. When I beheld this I sighed, and said within myself, "Surely mortal man is a broomstick!" Nature sent him into the world strong and lusty, in a thriving condition, wearing his own hair on his head, the proper branches of this reasoning vegetable, till the ax of intemperance has lopped off his green boughs, and left him a withered trunk; he then flies to art, and puts on a periwig, valuing himself upon an unnatural bundle of hairs, all covered with powder, that never grew on his head; but now should this our broomstick pretend to enter the scene, proud

[*] This essay is a satire on the writings of Robert Boyle.

of those birchen spoils it never bore, and all
covered with dust, through the sweepings of the
finest lady's chamber, we should be apt to rid-
icule and despise its vanity. Partial judges that
we are of our own excellences, and other men's
defaults!

But a broomstick, perhaps you will say, is an
emblem of a tree standing on its head; and pray
what is a man but a topsy-turvy creature, his
animal faculties perpetually mounted on his rational, his head where his heels should be, grovel-
ing on the earth? And yet, with all his faults,
he sets up to be a universal reformer and cor-
rector of abuses, a remover of grievances; rakes
into every slut's corner of nature, bringing hidden corruptions to the light; and raises a mighty
dust where there was none before, sharing deeply
all the while in the very same pollutions he
pretends to sweep away. His last days are spent
in slavery to women, and generally the least
deserving; till, worn to the stumps, like his
brother besom, he is either kicked out-of-doors,
or made use of to kindle flames for others to
warm themselves by.

V

GULLIVER AMONG THE GIANTS[5]

My mistress had a daughter of nine years old, a child of towardly parts for her age, very dexterous at her needle, and skilful in dressing her baby. Her mother and she contrived to fit up the baby's cradle for me against night; the cradle was put into a small drawer of a cabinet, and the drawer placed upon a hanging shelf for fear of the rats. This was my bed all the time I stayed with those people; tho made more convenient by degrees, as I began to learn their language and make my wants known. This young girl was so handy, that after I had once or twice pulled off my clothes before her, she was able to dress and undress me; tho I never gave her that trouble when she would let me do either myself. She made me seven shirts, and some other linen, of as fine cloth as could be got, which indeed was coarser than sackcloth; and these she constantly washed for me with her own hands. She was likewise my school-mistress, to teach me the language: when I pointed to anything, she told me the name of it in her own tongue; so that in a few days I was able to call for whatever I had a mind to. She was very good-natured, and not above forty

[5] From "Gulliver's Travels." At this point in the story Gulliver, shipwrecked in the country of Brobdingnag, had by the farmer who found him been given as a plaything to his little daughter Glumdalclitch, who, altho only nine years old, was forty feet tall.

feet high, being little for her age. She gave me the name of Grildrig, which the family took up, and afterwards the whole kingdom. The word imports what the Latins call *homunculus*, the Italians *homunceletino*, and the English *mannikin*. To her I chiefly owe my preservation in that country; we never parted while I was there: I called her my *Glumdalclitch*, or little nurse; and should be guilty of great ingratitude if I omitted this honorable mention of her care and affection toward me, which I heartily wish it lay in my power to requite as she deserves, instead of being the innocent but unhappy instrument of her disgrace, as I have too much reason to fear.

It now began to be known and talked of in the neighborhood that my master had found a strange animal in the field, about the bigness of a *splacnuck*, but exactly shaped in every part like a human creature, which it likewise imitated in all its actions: seemed to speak in a little language of its own, had already learned several words of theirs, went erect upon two legs, was tame and gentle, would come when it was called, do whatever it was bid, had the finest limbs in the world, and a complexion fairer than a nobleman's daughter of three years old.

Another farmer who lived hard by, and was a particular friend of my master, came on a visit on purpose to inquire into the truth of this story. I was immediately produced and placed upon a table, where I walked as I was commanded, drew my hanger, put it up again, made my reverence to my master's guest, asked him in his own language how he did, and told him he was welcome—just as my little nurse had instructed me. This man who was old and dim-sighted, put on his spectacles to behold me better; at which I could not forbear laughing very heartily, for his eyes appeared like the full moon shining into a chamber at two windows. Our people, who discovered the cause of my mirth, bore me company in laughing; at which the old fellow was fool enough to be angry and out of countenance. He had the character of a great miser; and to my misfortune, he well deserved it, by the cursed advice he gave my master to show me as a sight upon a market-day in the next town, which was half an hour's riding, about two-and-twenty miles from our house. I guessed there was some mischief contriving when I observed my master and his friend whispering long together, sometimes pointing at me; and my fears made me fancy that I overheard and understood some of their words.

But the next morning Glumdalclitch, my little nurse, told me the whole matter, which she had cunningly picked out from her mother. The poor girl laid me on her bosom, and fell a-weeping with shame and grief. She apprehended some mischief would happen to me from rude vulgar folks, who might squeeze me to death, or break one of my limbs by taking me in their hands. She had also observed how modest I was in my nature, how nicely I regarded my honor, and what an indignity I should conceive it to be exposed for money as a public spectacle to the meanest of the people. She said her papa and mama had promised that Grildrig should be hers; but now she found they meant to serve

232

her as they did last year, when they pretended to give her a lamb, and yet, as soon as it was fat, sold it to a butcher. For my own part, I may truly affirm that I was less concerned than my nurse. I had a strong hope, which never left me, that I should one day recover my liberty: and as to the ignominy of being carried about for a monster, I considered myself to be a perfect stranger in the country, and that such a misfortune could never be charged upon me as a reproach if ever I should return to England, since the King of Great Britain himself, in my condition, must have undergone the same distress.

My master, pursuant to the advice of his friend, carried me in a box the next market-day to the neighboring town, and took along with him his little daughter, my nurse, upon a pillion behind him. The box was close on every side, with a little door for me to go in and out, and a few gimlet-holes to let in air. The girl had been so careful as to put the quilt of her baby's bed into it for me to lie down on. However, I was terribly shaken and discomposed in this journey, tho it were but of half an hour; for the horse went about forty feet at every step, and trotted so high that the agitation was equal to the rising and falling of a ship in a great storm, but much more frequent. Our journey was somewhat farther than from London to St. Alban's. My master alighted at an inn which he used to frequent; and after consulting a while with the innkeeper, and making some necessary preparations, he hired the "grultrud," or crier, to give notice through the town of a strange creature to be seen at the sign of the Green

Eagle, not so big as a splacnuck (an animal in that country very finely shaped, about six feet long), and in every part of the body resembling a human creature—could speak several words, and perform a hundred diverting tricks.

I was placed upon a table in the largest room of the inn, which might be near three hundred feet square. My little nurse stood on a low stool close to the table, to take care of me and direct what I should do. My master, to avoid a crowd, would suffer only thirty people at a time to see me. I walked about on the table as the girl commanded; she asked me questions as far as she knew my understanding of the language reached, and I answered them as loud as I could. I turned about several times to the company, paid my humble respects, said "they were welcome," and used some other speeches I had been taught. I took up a thimble filled with liquor, which Glumdalclitch had given me for a cup, and drank their health. I drew out my hanger, and flourished with it after the manner of fencers in England. My nurse gave me a part of a straw, which I exercised as a pike, having learned the art in my youth. I was that day shown to twelve sets of company, and as often forced to act over again the same fopperies, till I was half dead with weariness and vexation; for those who had seen me made such wonderful reports that the people were ready to break down the doors to come in. My master, for his own interest, would not suffer any one to touch me except my nurse; and to prevent danger, benches were set round the table at such a distance as to put me out of everybody's reach. However, an unlucky schoolboy aimed a hazel-nut directly at my head, which very narrowly missed me; otherwise it came with so much violence that it would have infallibly knocked out my brains, for it was almost as large as a small pumpion: but I had the satisfaction to see the young rogue well beaten and turned out of the room. . . .

My master's design was to show me in all the towns by the way; and to step out of the road, for fifty or a hundred miles, to any village or person of quality's house where he might expect custom. We made easy journeys, of not above seven or eight score miles a day; for Glumdalclitch, on purpose to spare me, complained she was tired with the trotting of the horse. She often took me out of my box, at my own desire, to give me air and show me the country; but always held me fast by a leading-string. We passed over five or six rivers, many degrees broader and deeper than the Nile or the Ganges; and there was hardly a rivulet so small as the Thames at London Bridge. We were ten weeks in our journey, and I was shown in eighteen large towns, besides many villages and private families.

JOSEPH ADDISON

Born in 1672, died in 1719; educated at Oxford, where he wrote a Latin poem which brought him a pension of three hundred pounds; traveled on the Continent in 1699-1703; Under-secretary of State in 1706; Secretary to the Lord Lieutenant of Ireland in 1709; Secretary for Ireland in 1715; Secretary of State in 1717; married the Countess of Warwick in 1716; for his periodical, *The Spectator*, published daily from March 1st, 1711, to December 6th, 1712, wrote 274 papers; including the Sir Roger de Coverley papers; author of many other writings, among which "Cato: A Tragedy" is notable.

I

IN WESTMINSTER ABBEY[1]

WHEN I am in a serious humor, I very often walk by myself in Westminster Abbey; where the gloominess of the place, and the use to which it is applied, with the solemnity of the building, and the condition of the people who lie in it, are apt to fill the mind with a kind of melancholy, or rather thoughtfulness, that is not disagreeable. I yesterday passed a whole afternoon in the churchyard, the cloisters, and the church, amusing myself with the tombstones and inscriptions that I met with in those several regions of the dead. Most of them recorded nothing else of the buried person, but that he was born upon one day, and died upon another: the whole history of his life being comprehended in those

[1] From "The Spectator," No. 26.

two circumstances, that are common to all mankind. I could not but look upon these registers of existence, whether of brass or marble, as a kind of satire upon the departed persons, who had left no other memorial of them, but that they were born and that they died. They put one in mind of several persons mentioned in the battles of heroic poems, who have sounding names given them, for no other reason but that they may be killed, and are celebrated for nothing but being knocked on the head.

> Glaucumque, Mcdontaque, Thersilochumque.
> —Virg.

The life of these men is finely described in Holy Writ by "the path of an arrow," which is immediately closed up and lost.

Upon my going into the church, I entertained myself with the digging of a grave; and saw, in every shovelful of it that was thrown up, the fragment of a bone or skull intermixt with a kind of fresh moldering earth that some time or other had a place in the composition of a human body. Upon this I began to consider with myself, what innumerable multitudes of people lay confused together under the pavement of that ancient cathedral; how men and women, friends and enemies, priests and soldiers, monks and prebendaries, were crumbled amongst one another, and blended together in the same common mass; how beauty, strength and youth, with old age, weakness, and deformity, lay undistinguished in the same promiscuous heap of matter.

And having thus surveyed this great magazine of mortality, as it were in the lump, I examined it more particularly by the accounts which I found on several of the monuments which are raised in every quarter of that ancient fabric. Some of them were covered with such extravagant epitaphs, that, if it were possible for the dead person to be acquainted with them, he would blush at the praises which his friends have bestowed upon him. There are others so excessively modest, that they deliver the character of the person departed in Greek or Hebrew, and by that means are not understood once in a twelvemonth. In the poetical quarter, I found there were poets who had no monuments, and monuments which had no poets. I observed, indeed, that the present war had filled the church with many of these uninhabited monuments, which had been erected to the memory of persons whose bodies were perhaps buried in the plains of Blenheim, or in the bosom of the ocean.

I could not but be very much delighted with several modern epitaphs, which are written with great elegance of expression and justness of thought, and therefore do honor to the living as well as to the dead. As a foreigner is very apt to conceive an idea of the ignorance or politeness of a nation from the turn of their public monuments and inscriptions, they should be submitted to the perusal of men of learning and genius before they are put in execution. Sir Cloudesley Shovel's monument has very often given me great offense; instead of the brave, rough English Admiral, which was the distinguishing character of that plain, gallant man, he is represented on his tomb by the figure of a beau, drest in a long periwig, and reposing himself upon velvet cushions under a canopy of state. The inscription is answerable to the monument; for instead of celebrating the many remarkable actions he had performed in the service of his country, it acquaints us only with the manner of his death, in which it was impossible for him to reap any honor. The Dutch, whom we are apt to despise for want of genius, show an infinitely greater taste of antiquity and politeness in their buildings and works of this nature, than what we meet with in those of our own country. The monuments of their admirals, which have been erected at the public expense, represent them like themselves; and are adorned with rostral crowns and naval ornaments, with beautiful festoons of seaweed, shells, and coral.

But to return to our subject. I have left the repository of our English kings for the contemplation of another day, when I shall find my mind disposed for so serious an amusement. I know that entertainments of this nature are apt to raise dark and dismal thoughts in timorous minds and gloomy imaginations: but for my own part, tho I am always serious, I do not know what it is to be melancholy; and can therefore take a view of nature in her deep and solemn scenes, with the same pleasure as in her most gay and delightful ones. By this means, I can improve myself with those objects which others consider with terror. When I look upon the tombs of the great, every emotion of envy dies in me; when I read the epitaphs of the beautiful, every inordinate desire goes out; when I meet with the grief of parents upon a tombstone, my heart melts with compassion; when

I see the tomb of the parents themselves, I consider the vanity of grieving for those whom we must quickly follow; when I see kings lying by those who deposed them, when I consider rival wits placed side by side, or the holy men that divided the world with their contests and disputes, I reflect with sorrow and astonishment on the little competitions, factions, and debates of mankind. When I read the several dates of the tombs, of some that died yesterday, and some six hundred years ago, I consider that great day when we shall all of us be contemporaries, and make our appearance together.

II

WILL HONEYCOMB AND HIS MARRIAGE[9]

My friend Will Honeycomb values himself very much upon what he calls the knowledge of mankind, which has cost him many disasters in his youth; for Will reckons every misfortune that he has met with among the women, and every encounter among the men, as parts of his education, and fancies he should never have been the man he is, had he not broke windows, knocked down constables, disturbed honest people with his midnight serenades, and beat up Phryne's quarters, when he was a young fellow. The engaging in adventures of this nature, Will calls the studying of mankind, and terms this knowl-

[9] From Nos. 105 and 530 of "The Spectator."

edge of the town, the knowledge of the world. Will ingenuously confesses, that for half his life his head ached every morning with reading of men over night; and at present comforts himself under sundry infirmities with the reflection that without them he could not have been acquainted with the gallantries of the age. This Will looks upon as the learning of a gentleman, and regards all other kinds of science as the accomplishments of one whom he calls a scholar, a bookish man, or a philosopher.

For these reasons Will shines in a mixed company, where he has the discretion not to go out of his depth, and has often a certain way of making his real ignorance appear a seeming one. Our club, however, has frequently caught him tripping, at which times they never spare him. For as Will often insults us with the knowledge of the town, we sometimes take our revenge upon him by our knowledge of books.

He was last week producing two or three letters which he writ in his youth to a coquette lady. The raillery of them was natural, and well enough for a mere man of the town; but very unluckily, several of the words were wrong spelt. Will laughed this off at first as well as he could; but finding himself pushed on all sides, and especially by the Templar, he told us with a little passion that he never liked pedantry in spelling, and that he spelt like a gentleman and not like a scholar: upon this Will had recourse to his old topic of showing the narrow-spiritedness, the pride and ignorance, of pedants; which he carried so far, that, upon my retiring to my lodgings, I could not forbear throwing together such reflections as occurred to me upon that subject.

A man who has been brought up among books, and is able to talk of nothing else, is a very indifferent companion, and what we call a pedant. But, methinks, we should enlarge the title, and give it to every one that does not know how to think out of his profession and particular way of life.

What is a greater pedant than a mere man of the town? Bar him the play-houses, a catalog of the reigning beauties, and an account of a few fashionable distempers that have befallen him, and you strike him dumb. How many a pretty gentleman's knowledge lies all within the verge of the court! He will tell you the names of the principal favorites, repeat the shrewd sayings of a man of quality, whisper an intrigue that is not yet blown upon by common fame; or, if the sphere of his observation is a little larger than ordinary, will perhaps enter into all the incidents, turns, and revolutions in a game of ombre. When he has gone thus far, he has shown you the whole circle of his accomplishments, his parts are drained, and he is disabled from any further conversation. What are these but rank pedants? and yet these are the men who value themselves most on their exemption from the pedantry of colleges.

I might here mention the military pedant, who always talks in a camp, and is storming towns, making lodgments, and fighting battles from one end of the year to the other. Everything he speaks smells of gunpowder: if you take away his artillery from him, he has not a word to say

for himself. I might likewise mention the law
pedant, that is perpetually putting cases, re-
peating the transactions of Westminster Hall,
wrangling with you upon the most indifferent
circumstances of life, and not to be convinced
of the distance of a place, or of the most trivial
point in conversation, but by dint of argument.
The state pedant is wrapt up in news, and lost
in politics. If you mention either of the kings
of Spain or Poland, he talks very notably; but
if you go out of the Gazette, you drop him. In
short, a mere courtier, a mere soldier, a mere
scholar, a mere anything, is an insipid pedantic
character, and equally ridiculous.

Of all the species of pedants which I have
mentioned, the book pedant is much the most
supportable: he has at least an exercised understanding, and a head which is full tho confused,
so that a man who converses with him may often
receive from him hints of things that are worth
knowing, and what he may possibly turn to his
own advantage, tho they are of little use to the
owner. The worst kind of pedants among learned
men are such as are naturally endowed with a
very small share of common sense, and have read
a great number of books without taste or distinction. . . .

My friend Will Honeycomb, who was so un-
mercifully witty upon the women, in a couple of
letters which I lately communicated to the public,
has given the ladies ample satisfaction by mar-
rying a farmer's daughter; a piece of news which
came to our club by the last post. The Templar
is very positive that he has married a dairy-
maid; but Will, in his letter to me on this occa-

sion, sets the best face upon the matter that he can, and gives a more tolerable account of his spouse. I must confess I suspected something more than ordinary, when upon opening the letter I found that Will was fallen off from his former gaiety, having changed Dear Spec, which was his usual salute at the beginning of the letter, into *"My worthy friend,"* and subscribed himself at the latter end of it, at full length, William Honeycomb. In short, the gay, the loud, the vain Will Honeycomb, who had made love to every great fortune that has appeared in town for above thirty years together, and boasted of favors from ladies whom he had never seen, is at length wedded to a plain country girl.

His letter gives us the picture of a converted rake. The sober character of the husband is dashed with the man of the town, and enlivened with those little cant phrases which have made my friend Will often thought very pretty company. But let us hear what he says for himself.

My WORTHY FRIEND.

I question not but you, and the rest of my acquaintance, wonder that I, who have lived in the smoke and gallantries of the town for thirty years together, should all on a sudden grow fond of a country life. Had not my dog of a steward run away as he did, without making up his accounts, I had still been immersed in sin and sea-coal. But since my late forced visit to my estate, I am so pleased with it, that I am resolved to live and die upon it. I am every day abroad among my acres, and can scarce forbear filling my letter with breezes, shades, flowers, meadows, and purling streams. The simplicity of manners which I have heard you so often speak of, and which appears here in perfection, charms me wonderfully. As an instance of it, I must acquaint you, and by your means the whole club, that I have lately married one of my tenants' daughters. She is born of honest parents, and tho she has no portion she has a great deal of virtue. The natural sweetness and innocence of her behavior, the freshness of her complexion, the unaffected turn of her shape and person, shot me through and through every time I saw her, and did more execution upon me in grogram than the greatest beauty in town or court had ever done in brocade. In short, she is such a one as promises me a good heir to my estate; and if by her means I can not leave to my children what are falsely called the gifts of birth, high titles and alliances, I hope to convey to them the more real and valuable gifts of birth, strong bodies and healthy constitutions. As for your fine women, I need not tell thee that I know them. I have had my share in their graces, but no more of that. It shall be my business hereafter to live the life of an honest man, and to act as becomes the master of a family. I question not but I shall draw upon me the raillery of the town, and be treated to the tune of *"The Marriage-hater match'd"*; but I am prepared for it. I have been as witty upon others in my time. To tell thee truly, I saw such a tribe of fashionable young fluttering coxcombs shot up, that I did not think my post of an *homme de ruelle* any longer tenable. I felt a certain stiffness in my limbs, which entirely destroyed that jauntiness of air I was once master of. Besides, for I may now confess my age to thee, I have been eight and forty above these twelve years. Since my retirement into the country will make a vacancy in the club, I could wish you would fill up my place with my friend Tom Dapperwit. He has an infinite deal of fire, and knows the town. For my own part, as I have said before, I shall endeavor to live hereafter suitable to a man in my station, as a prudent head of a family, a good husband, a careful father (when it shall so happen), and as

Your most sincere friend and humble servant,

WILLIAM HONEYCOMB.

III

PRIDE OF BIRTH [*]

HORACE, Juvenal, Boileau, and indeed the greatest writers in almost every age, have exposed with all the strength of wit and good sense, the vanity of a man's valuing himself upon his ancestors, and endeavored to show that true nobility consists in virtue, not in birth. With submission, however, to so many great authorities, I think they have pushed this matter a little too far. We ought in gratitude to honor the posterity of those who have raised either the interest or reputation of their country, and by whose labors we ourselves are more happy, wise, or virtuous than we should have been without them. Besides, naturally speaking, a man bids fairer for great-

[*] From No. 137 of "The Guardian."

ness of soul, who is the descendant of worthy ancestors, and has good blood in his veins, than one who is come of an ignoble and obscure parentage. For these reasons, I think a man of merit, who is derived from an illustrious line, is very justly to be regarded more than a man of equal merit who has no claim to hereditary honors. Nay, I think those who are indifferent in themselves, and have nothing else to distinguish them but the virtues of their forefathers, are to be looked upon with a degree of veneration even upon that account, and to be more respected than the common run of men who are of low and vulgar extraction.

After having thus ascribed due honors to birth and parentage, I must, however, take notice of those who arrogate to themselves more honors than are due to them upon this account. The first are such who are not enough sensible that vice and ignorance taint the blood, and that an unworthy behavior degrades and disennobles a man in the eyes of the world, as much as birth and family aggrandize and exalt him.

The second are those who believe a *new* man of an elevated merit is not more to be honored than an insignificant and worthless man who is descended from a long line of patriots and heroes; or, in other words, behold with contempt a person who is such a man as the first founder of their family was, upon whose reputation they value themselves.

But I shall chiefly apply myself to those whose quality sits uppermost in all their discourses and behavior. An empty man of a great family is a creature that is scarce conversible. You read his ancestry in his smile, in his air, in his eyebrow. He has, indeed, nothing but his nobility to give employment to his thoughts. Rank and precedency are the important points which he is always discussing within himself. A gentleman of this turn began a speech in one of King Charles's parliaments: "Sir, I had the honor to be born at a time"—upon which a rough, honest gentleman took him up short, "I would fain know what that gentleman means: is there any one in this house that has *not* had the honor to be born as well as himself?" The good sense which reigns in our nation has pretty well destroyed this starched behavior among men who have seen the world, and know that every gentleman will be treated upon a foot of equality. But there are many who have had their education among women, dependents or flatterers, that lose all the respect which would otherwise be paid them by being too assiduous in procuring it.

My Lord Froth has been so educated in punctilio, that he governs himself by a ceremonial in all the ordinary occurrences of life. He measures out his bow to the degree of the person he converses with. I have seen him in every inclination of the body, from a familiar nod to the low stoop in the salutation-sign. I remember five of us, who were acquainted with one another, met together one morning at his lodgings, when a wag of the company was saying, it would be worth while to observe how he would distinguish us at his first entrance. Accordingly, he no sooner came into the room, but, casting his eye about, "My lord such a one (says he) your most humble servant.—Sir Richard, your humble servant.—Your servant, Mr. Ironside.—Mr. Ducker, how do you do?—Hah! Frank, are you there?''

There is nothing more easy than to discover a man whose head is full of his family. Weak minds that have imbibed a strong tincture of the nursery, younger brothers that have been brought up to nothing, superannuated retainers to a great house, have generally their thoughts taken up with little else.

I had some years ago an aunt of my own, by name Mrs. Martha Ironside, who would never marry beneath herself, and is supposed to have died a maid in fourscorth year of her age. She was the chronicle of our family, and passed away the greatest part of the last forty years of her life in recounting the antiquity, marriages, exploits, and alliances of the Ironsides. Mrs. Martha conversed generally with a knot of old virgins, who were likewise of good families, and had been very cruel all the beginning of the last century. They were every one of them as proud as Lucifer, but said their prayers twice a day, and in all other respects were the best women in the world. If they saw a fine petticoat at church, they immediately took to pieces the pedigree of her that wore it, and would lift up their eyes to heaven at the confidence of the saucy minx, when they found she was an honest tradesman's daughter. It is impossible to describe the pious indignation that would rise in them at the sight of a man who lived plentifully on an estate of his own getting. They were transported with zeal beyond measure, if they heard of a young woman's matching into a great family upon account only of her beauty, her

merit, or her money. In short, there was not a
female within ten miles of them that was in
possession of a gold watch, a pearl necklace, or
a piece of Mechlin lace, but they examined her
title to it.

My aunt Martha used to chide me very frequently for not sufficiently valuing myself. She
would not eat a bit all dinner-time, if at an
invitation she found she had been seated below
herself; and would frown upon me for an hour
together, if she saw me give place to any man
under a baronet. As I was once talking to her
of a wealthy citizen whom she had refused in
her youth, she declared to me with great warmth,
that she preferred a man of quality in his shirt
to the richest man upon the change in a coach
and six. She pretended that our family was
nearly related by the mother's side to half a
dozen peers; but as none of them knew anything
of the matter, we always kept it as a secret
among ourselves. A little before her death, she
was reciting to me the history of my forefathers;
but dwelling a little longer than ordinary upon
the actions of Sir Gilbert Ironside, who had a
horse shot under him at Edgehill fight, I gave an
unfortunate *pish!* and asked, "What was all
this to me?" upon which she retired to her
closet and fell a-scribbling for three hours together; in which time, as I afterwards found,
she struck me out of her will, and left all that
she had to my sister Margaret, a wheedling baggage, that used to be asking questions about her
great-grandfather from morning to night. She
now lies buried among the family of the Ironsides, with a stone over her, acquainting the

reader that she died at the age of eighty years, a spinster, and that she was descended of the ancient family of the Ironsides; after which follows the genealogy drawn up by her own hand.

IV

SIR ROGER AND HIS HOME *

THE first of our society is a gentleman of Worcestershire, of ancient descent, a baronet, his name Sir Roger de Coverley. His great-grandfather was inventor of that famous country-dance which is called after him. All who know that shire are very well acquainted with the parts and merits of Sir Roger. He is a gentleman that is very singular in his behavior; but his singularities proceed from his good sense, and are contradictions to the manners of the world only as he thinks the world is in the wrong. However, this humor creates him no enemies, for he does nothing with sourness or obstinacy; and his being unconfined to modes and forms makes him but the readier and more capable to please and oblige all who know him. When he is in town he lives in Soho Square. It is said, he keeps himself a bachelor, by reason he was crossed in love by a perverse beautiful widow

* From Nos. 2 and 106 of "The Spectator." It has been conjectured that the world owes to Steele rather than to Addison the original conception of the character of Sir Roger, altho its development was due more largely to Addison.

of the next county to him. Before this disappointment, Sir Roger was what you call a fine gentleman; had often supped with my Lord Rochester and Sir George Etherege, fought a duel upon his first coming to town, and kicked Bully Dawson in a public coffee-house, for calling him youngster. But, being ill used by the abovementioned widow, he was very serious for a year and a half; and tho, his temper being naturally jovial, he at last got over it, he grew careless of himself and never drest afterward. He continues to wear a coat and doublet of the same cut that were in fashion at the time of his repulse, which, in his merry humors he tells us, has been in and out twelve times since he first wore it. He is now in his fifty-sixth year, cheerful, gay, and hearty; keeps a good house both in town and country; a great lover of mankind; but there is such a mirthful cast in his behavior that he is rather beloved than esteemed. His tenants grow rich, his servants look satisfied, all the young women profess love to him, and the young men are glad of his company; when he comes into a house, he calls the servants by their names, and talks all the way up-stairs to a visit. I must not omit that Sir Roger is a justice of the *quorum;* that he fills the chair at a quarter-session with great abilities, and three months ago gained universal applause by explaining a passage in the Game Act.

Having often received an invitation from my friend Sir Roger de Coverley to pass away a month with him in the country, I last week accompanied him thither, and am settled with him for some time at his country-house, where I

intend to form several of my ensuing specula-
tions. Sir Roger, who is very well acquainted
with my humor, lets me rise and go to bed when
I please; dine at his own table or in my chamber, as I think fit; sit still and say nothing without bidding me be merry. When the gentlemen
of the country come to see him, he only shows
me at a distance: as I have been walking in his
fields, I have observed them stealing a sight of
me over an hedge, and have heard the knight
desiring them not to let me see them, for that
I hated to be stared at.

I am the more at ease in Sir Roger's family,
because it consists of sober and staid persons:
for, as the knight is the best master in the world,
he seldom changes his servants; and, as he is
beloved by all about him, his servants never
care for leaving him; by this means his domestics are all in years, and grown old with their
master. You would take his valet-de-chambre
for his brother; his butler is gray-headed; his
groom is one of the gravest men that I have
ever seen; and his coachman has the looks of
a privy-councillor. You see the goodness of the
master even in the old house-dog, and in a gray
pad that is kept in the stable with great care
and tenderness, out of regard to his past services,
tho he has been useless for several years.

I could not but observe with a great deal of
pleasure the joy that appeared in the countenance
of these ancient domestics upon my friend's arrival at his country-seat. Some of them could
not refrain from tears at the sight of their old
master; every one of them prest forward to do
something for him, and seemed discouraged if

they were not employed. At the same time the good old knight, with a mixture of the father and the master of the family, tempered the inquiries after his own affairs with several kind questions relating to themselves. This humanity and good-nature engages everybody to him, so that, when he is pleasant upon any of them, all his family are in good humor, and none so much as the person whom he diverts himself with: on the contrary, if he coughs, or betrays any infirmity of old age, it is easy for a stander-by to observe a secret concern in the looks of all his servants.

My worthy friend has put me under the particular care of his butler, who is a very prudent man, and, as well as the rest of his fellow servants, wonderfully desirous of pleasing me, because they have often heard their master talk of me as of his particular friend.

My chief companion, when Sir Roger is diverting himself in the woods or the fields, is a very venerable man who is ever with Sir Roger, and has lived at his house in the nature of a chaplain above thirty years. This gentleman is a person of good sense and some learning, of a very regular life and obliging conversation: he heartily loves Sir Roger, and knows that he is very much in the old knight's esteem, so that he lives in the family rather as a relation than a dependent.

I have observed in several of my papers, that my friend Sir Roger, amidst all his good qualities, is something of a humorist; and that his virtues, as well as imperfections, are, as it were, tinged by a certain extravagance, which makes them particularly his, and distinguishes them from those of other men. This cast of mind, as it is generally very innocent in itself, so it renders his conversation highly agreeable, and more delightful than the same degree of sense and virtue would appear in their common or ordinary colors. As I was walking with him last night, he asked me how I liked the good man whom I have just now mentioned; and, without staying for my answer, told me that he was afraid of being insulted with Latin and Greek at his own table; for which reason he desired a particular friend of his at the university to find him out a clergyman rather of plain sense than much learning, of a good aspect, a clear voice, a sociable temper, and if possible a man that understood a little about backgammon. "My friend," says Sir Roger, "found me out this gentleman, who, besides the endowments required of him, is, they tell me, a good scholar, tho he does not show it. I have given him the parsonage of the parish; and, because I know his value, have settled upon him a good annuity for life. If he outlives me, he shall find that he was higher in my esteem than perhaps he thinks he is. He has now been with me thirty years; and, tho he does not know I have taken notice of it, has never in all that time asked anything of me for himself, tho he is every day soliciting me for something in behalf of one or other of my tenants, his parishioners.

END OF VOLUME III